# Architecture

# Architecture

Written by Philip Wilkinson

in collaboration with Adam Reed Tucker

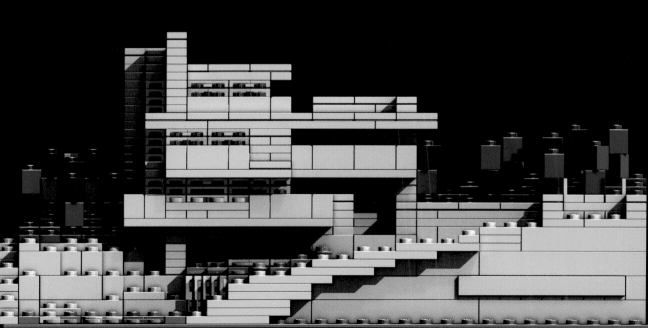

# CONTENTS

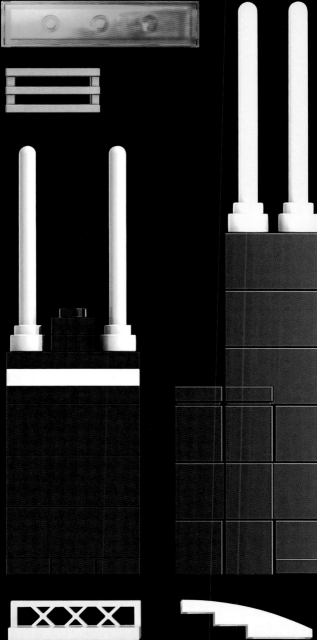

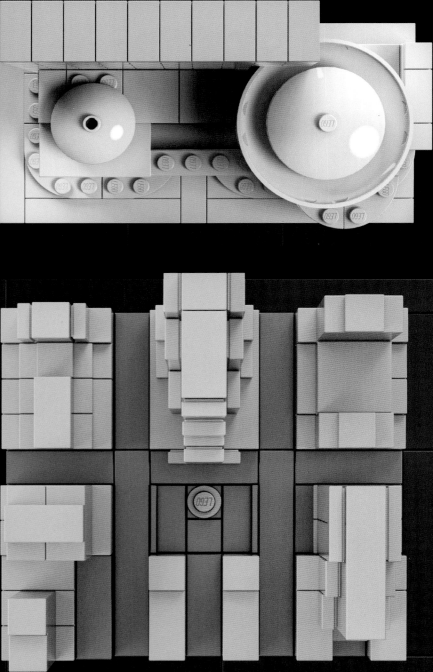

# FOREWORD

by Adam Reed Tucker

When I think about what architecture is, or more importantly why architecture is such an integral part of our lives, I cannot help but be reminded of when I was a child learning to stack simple wooden blocks. Was it the placement of shapes was negotiating or rather the relationship of their colours? Perhaps it was both.

Architecture can be an extremely challenging profession to master, but at its core it is simply the arrangement of various shapes and colours – the same techniques we learn as an infant, stacking blocks and LEGO® bricks. It is this founding principle that defines the basis of my particular philosophy in architectural design theory. am drawn to the ability to break down a complex form into its pure basics and conversely, to create a sophisticated design from simple building blocks.

The LEGO brick is my way of illustrating my creativity. I use it in order to physically and visually demonstrate what architecture is – through my eyes. Whether recreating a world famous landmark or inventing something completely original utilise the LEGO brick as a creative medium to capture the essence of its design

There are many ways to express yourself visually, but architects must think and create in three dimensions and what could be more perfect to work with than LEGO bricks? At their essence, they are 3D shapes that come in many colours They do not require glue or cutting, and nor do they require a skillful hand to use them. Therein lies the magic of the LEGO brick.

t is in this way that I discovered I could share architecture with the world allowing it to be embraced without intimidation. LEGO Architecture was developed through my shared vision with the LEGO Group to allow everyone to experience understand and enjoy architecture through a medium that pretty much everybody can relate to. This book explores the creative journey behind each LEGO Architecture model, the techniques used to create the models and the inks between the models and the iconic buildings and structures they were based on. As illustrated here, the LEGO brick has almost endless possibilities, and the application of this medium can only continue to grow as the world carries on building and the builders of tomorrow look back on the incredible architecture that has shaped our world.

# INTRODUCTION

The story of LEGO® Architecture goes back to the early 1960s, a time when LEGO products were increasing in popularity around the world and the company was looking to increase still further the potential and scope of the LEGO brick. One idea they came up with was very simple. Until this time, the system had been based firmly on the brick, but the LEGO designers came up with an element that was the same as a brick, but just one third of a brick's height – they had invented the plate.

Plates made it easier to build more detailed models, including buildings in a modern architectural style. The variety of white elements suited this style well too. The result was a new range – the Scale Model series, which encouraged people to design dream houses.

The invention of plates and the idea that models could be built to scale did not just appeal to LEGO enthusiasts. Architects, who were used to making scale models of their buildings with more conventional materials, liked it too. A number of architects in the 1960s and 1970s made models of their projects in LEGO bricks. A celebrated example was Britain's Owen Luder Partnership, which used a LEGO model when designing a 1970s scheme to redevelop Hay's Wharf on the south bank of the Thames in London. Canadian-Israeli architect Moshe Safdie also used LEGO bricks when designing Habitat 67, his famous housing scheme in Montreal.

The LEGO Scale Model series was phased out in the mid-1960s. However, the plate remained a key part of the assortment of LEGO bricks, and as the LEGO range and the number of components grew, users did not stop making architectural models. As well as individual enthusiasts, some architects still saw the potential of the LEGO brick to make models to capture their ideas in 3D and catch the eye of the public. The Danish architectural firm Bjarke Ingels Group (BIG) was one with their LEGO Towers project, exhibited in New York in 2007.

One of the architects who saw the potential of LEGO bricks was Chicago-based Adam Reed Tucker. He began to make large one-off models of landmark buildings in 2006, quickly catching the eye of the LEGO community with models of New York's Empire State Building and other skyscrapers, some of which were more than 2 metres tall. When members of the LEGO team saw these models, they were impressed, and grasped the potential for producing smaller models of real buildings – models that architecture enthusiasts and others would be able to buy and build.

The LEGO Group's designers began to work with Adam Reed Tucker, who designed smaller scale models of Chicago's Sears Tower (now the Willis Tower) and John Hancock Center. Launched in 2008, they marked the beginning of the LEGO Architecture series. The series now includes more than 20 models. In addition, the LEGO Group has launched a set called LEGO Architecture Studio. Consisting entirely of white components, the set is aimed at people who want to build their own designs and explore the principles of architecture. Meanwhile, the Architecture series itself goes from strength to strength, with an impressive variety of models available to LEGO enthusiasts all over the world.

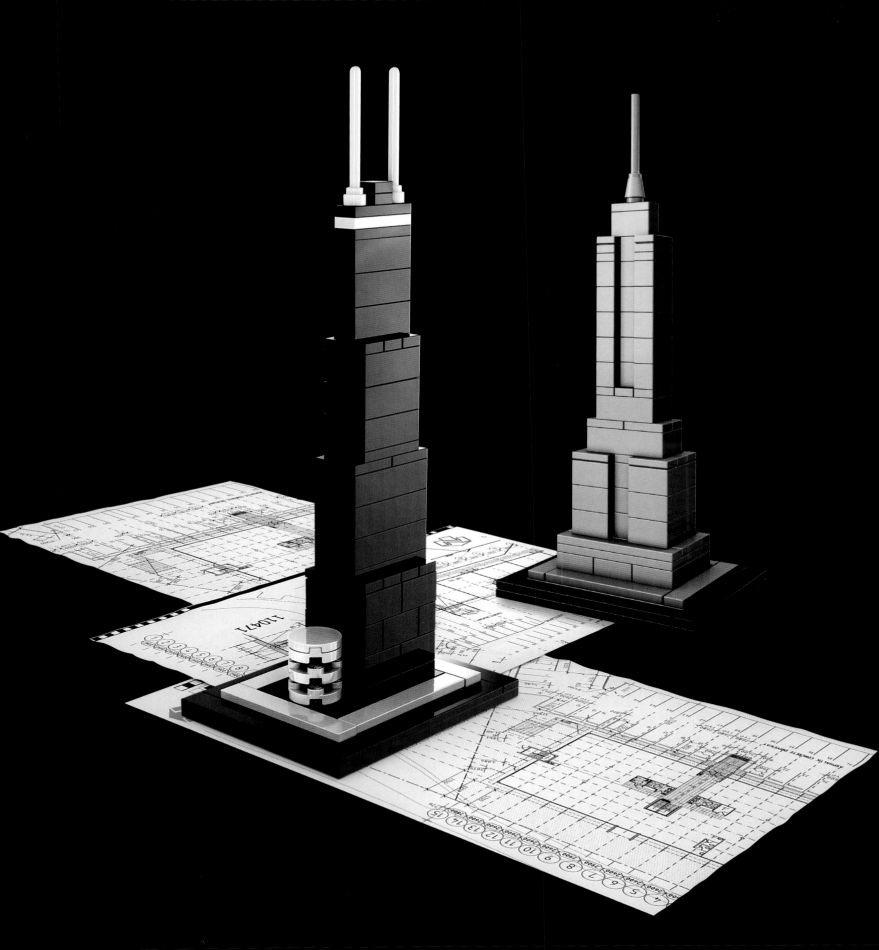

**Willis Tower**
**Model N°**
**21000**

**Empire State**
**Building**
**Model N°**
**21002**

**The White House**
**Model N° 21006**

**Brandenburg Gate**
**Model N° 21011**

**John Hancock**
**Center**
**Model N°**
**21001**

**Seattle Space**
**Needle**
**Model N°**
**21003**

**Rockefeller**
**Center®**
**Model N°**
**21007**

**2008**   **2009**   **2010**   **2011**

**Farnsworth**
**House™**
**Model N°**
**21009**

**Fallingwater®**
**Model N° 21005**

**Solomon R.**
**Guggenheim**
**Museum®**
**Model N° 21004**

**Robie™ House**
**Model N° 21010**

**Burj Khalifa**
**Model N° 21008**

**Sungnyemun Gate**
**Model N°**
**21016**

**The Leaning Tower of Pisa**
**Model N°**
**21015**

**The Trevi Fountain**
**Model N° 21020**

**Big Ben**
**Model N°**
**21013**

**United Nations Headquarters**
**Model N° 21018**

**The Eiffel Tower**
**Model N°**
**21019**

# 2012

# 2013

# 2014

**Villa Savoye**
**Model N° 21014**

**Marina Bay Sands®**
**Model N°**
**21021**

# LEGO® ARTIST PROFILE

## Adam Reed Tucker

Adam Reed Tucker's combined passions for architecture and LEGO bricks has become a global enterprise.

Chicago-based Adam Reed Tucker was working as an architect in 2006, when the real-estate recession brought about a turning-point in his career. Looking for an alternative to architecture, he considered his career options and what he most liked to do. He decided that he wanted to work with his hands and, remembering how much he enjoyed making models of buildings in architecture school, decided to resume making scale models of buildings.

After the tragic events of 9/11, Adam Reed Tucker noticed that visitor numbers to tall buildings in the USA had gone dramatically down. Creating models seemed like a good way of reconnecting people with icons of US architecture such as the Empire State Building. However, rather than regular sculptor's materials, Adam wanted to use a medium that was accessible to many people. LEGO® bricks, which involve no gluing, no cutting and no carving, seemed ideal.

In 2006, Adam visited a branch of Toys R Us, filled 11 shopping carts with LEGO sets, and set about refamiliarising himself with the bricks that he had played with as

Adam began playing with LEGO bricks as a boy, when an aunt bought him his first LEGO set.

Adam at work is his studio: he consults a reference book while working on the LEGO model of the Solomon R. Guggenheim Museum® in New York.

Adam took his models to events run by the LEGO community. These large models, including an Empire State Building some 2 metres tall, attracted the attention of the team from the LEGO Group's New Business Group. They were impressed with the imposing, one-off models and saw the potential for creating smaller models that customers would want to build for themselves. So Adam began working on models of a range of buildings, on a smaller scale but retaining the integrity of the larger works.

Beginning with buildings in the American Midwest, Adam cast his net wider, taking in structures on the east and west coasts of the U.S. and then still further afield. As well as a huge amount of creative time, this process of developing the first models also involved a great deal of contact with the owners of the buildings. Adam got their approval of the projects and persuaded them to grant licensing agreements with the LEGO Group and with potential retailers who would stock the models in their stores. Adam formed a company, Brickstructures Inc., through which he continues to create one-off large-scale models. Meanwhile, through the worldwide sales of the LEGO Architecture series itself, one man's project has turned into a global enterprise that continues to enthrall LEGO buyers and model-builders all over the world.

Thousands of LEGO bricks are stored in Adam's Chicago studio.

# LEGO® ARTIST & BUILDER PROFILES

## Steen Sig Andersen

Steen Sig Andersen has worked as a LEGO® builder and designer for more than 30 years. Over this period he has worked on a wide variety of different models, including many in the City, Castle and Space ranges. He has also spent three years in the company's Show and Events department, making one-off large-scale exhibition models of animals, buildings and other subjects, including a version of the Pompidou Centre, Paris, at 1:100 scale. Immediately before working on the LEGO Architecture series, he worked on LEGO Creator. Over his long career, Steen has worked on well over 100 models. Among his favourites have been the Eiffel Tower, Volkswagen Beetle, Grand Carousel and Winter Village Post Office.

**LEGO builder: Steen Sig Andersen**

## Rok Zgolin Kobe

Rok Zgalin Kobe played with LEGO bricks as a child, having inherited his first LEGO sets from his mother. Building LEGO models and developing his drawing skills helped to shape his career choice and he studied architecture at the University of Ljubljana. At university, he realised that the best way to see his designs was to create models. Eventually, Rok and his wife Ana set up an architectural practice in Slovenia, while Rok also returned to university to write a doctoral thesis. Then the opportunity came to combine his love of LEGO building with his professional work. Since then he has enjoyed collaborating with the LEGO Architecture team to create five models: the Imperial Hotel, the UN Headquarters, Eiffel Tower,

**LEGO artist: Rok Zgolin Kobe**

# Jørn Kristian Thomsen

As a child, Jørn enjoyed building additional features into his LEGO models – . for example, he made cars with motors driven by elastic bands. After school he worked as an electrician, which helped to develop his interest in inventing things and finding new solutions to practical problems. In his spare time, he built a remote control into a LEGO train. In the late 1980s, he joined the LEGO Group and has since worked on 75 LEGO sets. Among his favourites are many Western and Mindstorms sets. During his 27 years at the LEGO Group, Jørn has liked creating toys that appeal to both children and adults. In his work on the LEGO Architecture series Jørn has loved the challenge of getting the models to look as much like the real buildings as possible, and the chance to use LEGO elements in interesting new ways.

**LEGO builder: Jørn Kristian Thomsen**

# Michael Hepp

Michael Hepp trained as a chef, then as a carpenter and designer, before deciding to study architecture at the Cologne University of Applied Science. Although he has had a very diverse career, there is a thread that links all these occupations – the chance they have given him to work with his hands. This is also true of Michael's work as a LEGO artist, which he sees in terms of discovering and interpreting buildings through the medium

# THE CREATIVE PROCESS

Site visits allow the artist to compare a model with the real building – and possibly make adjustments to the design.

All the models in the LEGO® Architecture series are of famous buildings and landmarks, but the designer of a LEGO model still has to examine the original buildings really closely, and look at measured drawings and plans to get a clear sense of the structure's size and all its features. The artist and builder pay particular attention to features such as the different building materials used, the colour and texture of walls and the size and shape of important elements such as doorways and windows.

The artist also has to make decisions about scale – is the model going to be a relatively simple creation at a small scale or a more complex, large-scale model? Sometimes, the precise choice of scale will depend on finding the best LEGO brick for a key part of the building. For example, the choice of 1x1 bricks for the white columns of the Farnsworth House™ dictated that the rest of the structure had to be a certain size.

When these basic decisions have been made, the artist tries them out. This process often involves working directly with LEGO bricks to make trial versions of the model, but the artist can also use the computer design program LEGO Digital Designer to assemble virtual models on-screen and may try out ideas by sketching

Consulting reference material is an important part of the creative process.

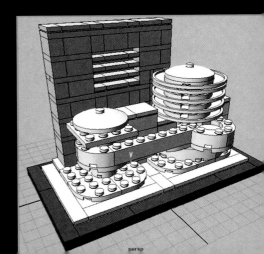

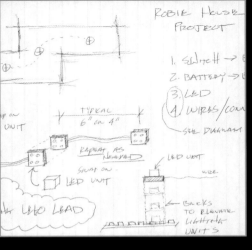

Pencil sketches are often used for jotting down ideas, such as this plan to light the interior of the Robie™ House model.

the project. Sometimes, as with the Eiffel Tower model, there is a close collaboration between artist and builder during the development stage, but in other cases the builder gets involved later on.

It is the builder's job to ensure that the artist's ideas are translated effectively into LEGO bricks to make a structure that is buildable and structurally sound, and that the instructions are not too difficult to follow. This may involve changing some of the LEGO parts, or adding elements to make the structure stronger.

The builder may also change the colour of some of the LEGO bricks – particularly ones that cannot be seen in the finished model. The reason for this is to make the diagrams in the instruction booklet easier to follow. When building some models, it can be difficult to work out which side of the half-completed model is which, so adding a brightly coloured brick or tile on one side makes it immediately easy to orientate the model. This technique was employed by artist Michael Hepp and builder Steen Sig Andersen in the model of the Villa Savoye, where there are red and blue tiles concealed in the base, to help the user to identify the sides of this almost square model.

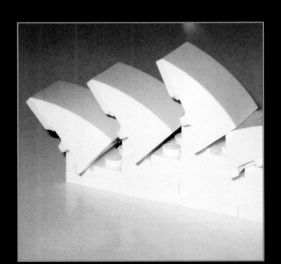

# FALLINGWATER® IN DEVELOPMENT

The LEGO® Architecture model of Frank Lloyd Wright's Fallingwater® was released in 2009 and so was one of the early models in the LEGO Architecture series, and the largest at the time it came out. It was designed by Adam Reed Tucker, who began by creating a simple 63-element model in grey and beige bricks to develop his concept of making the model slot together like a Japanese puzzle box. Having shown this model to the experts at the Frank Lloyd Wright Foundation, he built a very large and much more complex version, made up of hundreds of LEGO bricks, so that he could work out the proportions of the building and the way its structure is put together. Having worked out the details, such as how to form the base and the foundation of the house, Adam finally created the finished model, using 811 LEGO bricks that were mainly grey and beige.

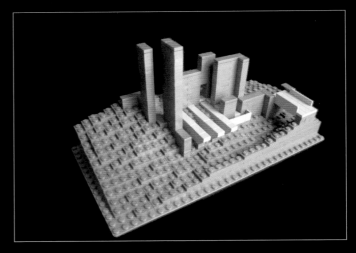

1. At the core of the initial model was a structure of grey bricks representing the stone walls that support the lower levels of the house and rise up through the building.

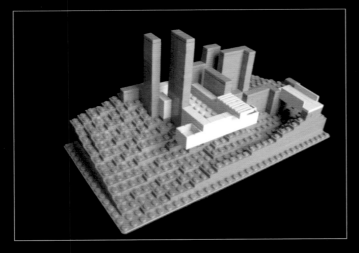

2. The small model was then built up in a series of beige sections that fitted together, starting with the lower levels.

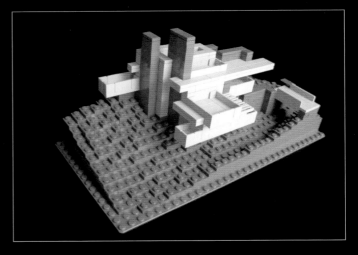

3. The upper levels slotted in above the lower levels, the balconies protruding as they do on the real building.

The large one-off model was built at a scale that allowed quite a lot of detail to be shown. Transparent tiles made up the windows and elements such as the outside steps were recreated.

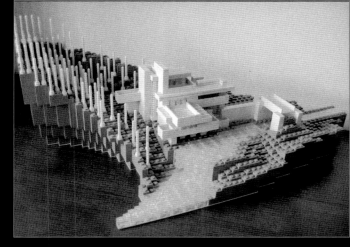

One idea was to use slender aerial elements to represent the trees that surround the house.

It was especially important to work out the foundations. The artist was influenced in part by the structure of the underlying masonry of the real house.

The artist tried various approaches to the surrounding rocky terrain and river, including using mainly white and grey bricks.

# LEGO® CITYSCAPE IN SCALE

- John Hancock Tower
  188 mm
- Willis Tower
  210 mm
- Empire State Building
  172 mm
- Seattle Space Needle
  227 mm
- Solomon R. Guggenheim Museum®
  101 mm
- Fallingwater®
  116 mm

- Brandenburg Gate
  88 mm
- Sydney Opera House™
  70 mm
- Big Ben
  193 mm
- Villa Savoye
  91 mm
- Sungnyemun
  107 mm
- Leaning Tower of Pisa
  260 mm

The name and shape of Sydney Opera House are trade marks of the Sydney Opera House Trust.

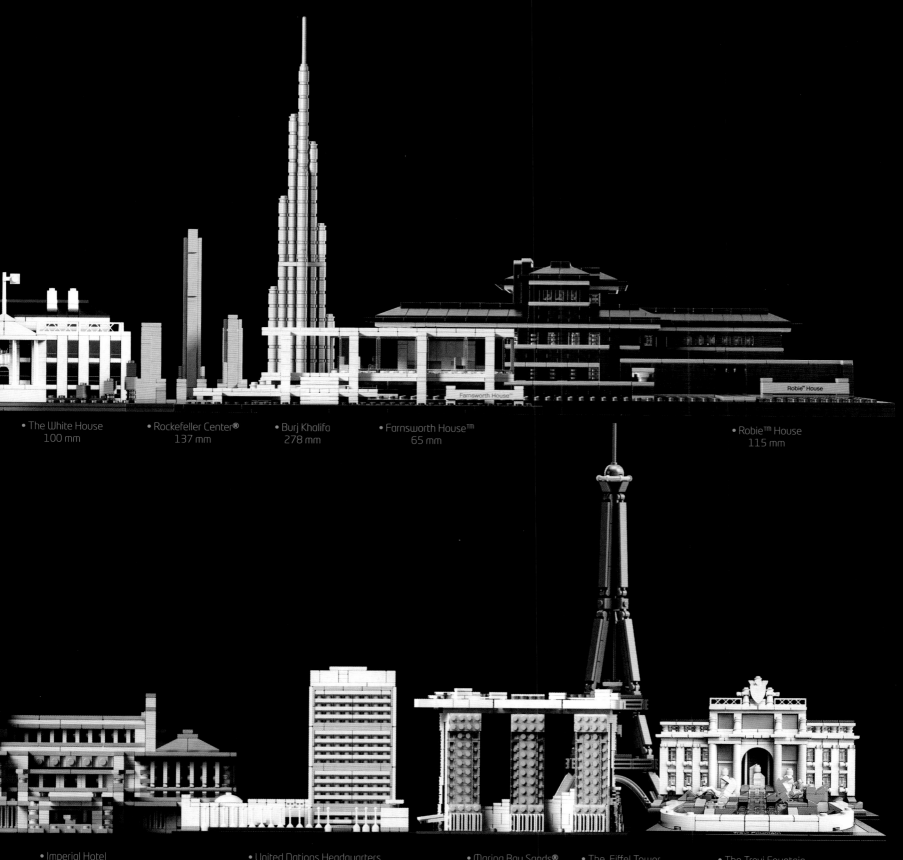

• The White House
100 mm

• Rockefeller Center®
137 mm

• Burj Khalifa
278 mm

• Farnsworth House™
65 mm

• Robie™ House
115 mm

• Imperial Hotel
108 mm

• United Nations Headquarters
138 mm

• Marina Bay Sands®
136 mm

• The Eiffel Tower
317 mm

• The Trevi Fountain
104 mm

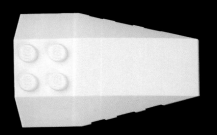

4x6 brick with
bow and angle

1x4 LEGO®
Technic brick

1x4x1⅓ brick
with curved top

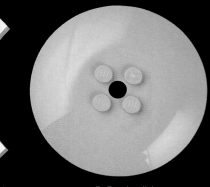

6x6 radar dish

4x4 brick with
bow and angle

1x1 slope

1x2 LEGO
Technic brick

1x1 LEGO
Technic brick

2x2 turntable plate

¼x4x1 bow
brick

1x2 hinge plate

# GLOSSARY

These are some of the types of LEGO® bricks and elements used in
the LEGO Architecture models. A classic 2x3 brick is perfect for the
walls of a sleek, modernist building, but there are many different
bricks and elements that are required for replicating windows, roofs,
and some more complex architectural shapes and features. LEGO
elements are often reappropriated from their usual role, for example
a fence element can be used for decorative lattice work on a portico,
or a lightsaber blade can double up as an elegant pillar.

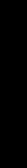

Bar

4x4 round plate

2x2 round plate

2x2 jumper plate

1x2 jumper plate

2x2 plate with
vertical snap

2x4 tile

2x2 round brick

1x5 tile

2x2 round tile

1x1 round tile

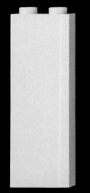

1x2x5 brick

1x1x5 brick

Mini shield

1x1x1 wall
corner

1x1 plate with
vertical clip

1x2 plate
with slide

3x4 slope

1x4x⅔ plate with bow

1x2x1 wall element

1x4x1 lattice fence

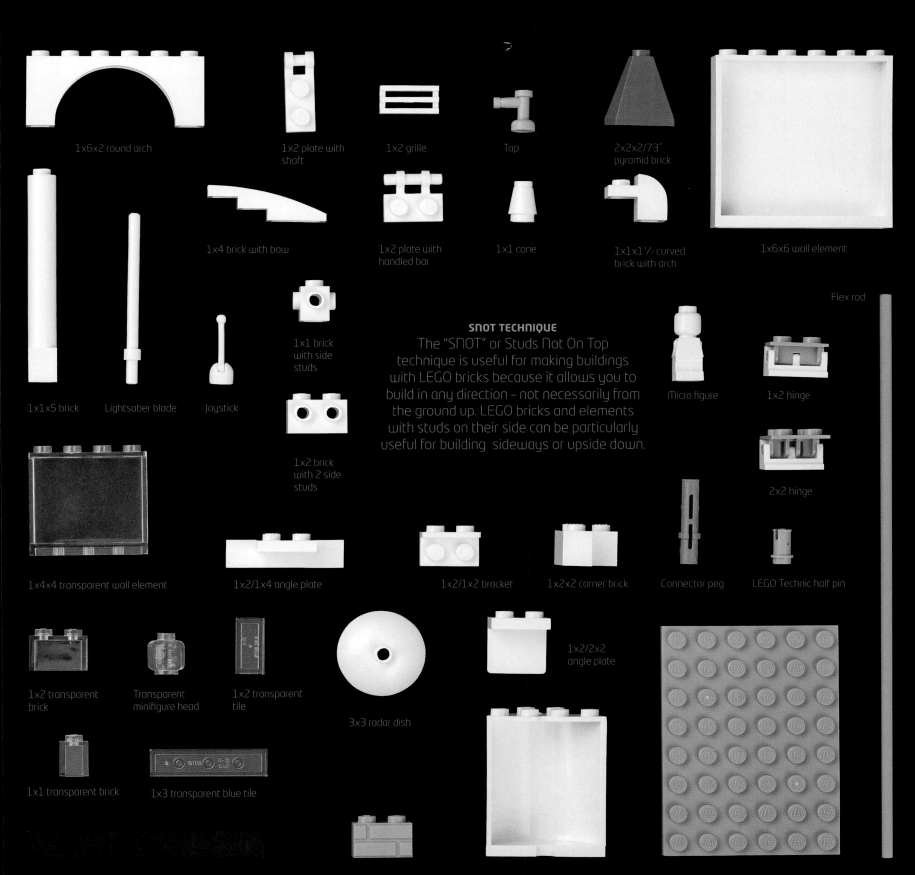

1x6x2 round arch

1x2 plate with shaft

1x2 grille

Tap

2x2x2/73° pyramid brick

1x4 brick with bow

1x2 plate with handled bar

1x1 cone

1x1x1½ curved brick with arch

1x6x6 wall element

1x1x5 brick

Lightsaber blade

Joystick

1x1 brick with side studs

1x2 brick with 2 side studs

Flex rod

Micro figure

1x2 hinge

2x2 hinge

## SNOT TECHNIQUE

The "SNOT" or Studs Not On Top technique is useful for making buildings with LEGO bricks because it allows you to build in any direction – not necessarily from the ground up. LEGO bricks and elements with studs on their side can be particularly useful for building sideways or upside down.

**23**

1x4x4 transparent wall element

1x2/1x4 angle plate

1x2/1x2 bracket

1x2x2 corner brick

Connector peg

LEGO Technic half pin

1x2 transparent brick

Transparent minifigure head

1x2 transparent tile

3x3 radar dish

1x2/2x2 angle plate

6x8 plate

1x1 transparent brick

1x3 transparent blue tile

1x6 tile

1x2 brick with embossed bricks

Round 2x2x4 wall element

# SOLOMON R. GUGGENHEIM MUSEUM®

## A Building of Two Parts

The model uses LEGO bricks of two main colours – white for the original structure designed by Frank Lloyd Wright, and beige for the annexe, as originally envisioned in Wright's perspective drawing. The annexe building was constructed in 1990–92 and was designed by Gwathmey Siegel and Associates. The annexe houses additional galleries and acts as a dramatic backdrop for the Wright-designed Museum. The model reflects this balance between the two elements of the Museum – the Wright building with all its curves, and the rectilinear lines of the Gwathmey Siegel building.

# SOLOMON R. GUGGENHEIM MUSEUM®

**LEGO® Artist: Adam Reed Tucker**

New York's Guggenheim Museum is one of the most iconic buildings designed by Frank Lloyd Wright. Its unmistakable presence on 5th Avenue features a spiralling "drum" shape that contains the main art gallery. Its soft, curving lines accentuate the horizontal buildings and skyscrapers that are the focus of the New York skyline. The Guggenheim is curvaceous, and when the museum was suggested to Adam Reed Tucker as a candidate for inclusion in the LEGO® Architecture series, he thought that it would be impossible to model the building using the available LEGO bricks. However, the artist's approach is not to copy the buildings literally and his background in design theory had taught him that there are ways of symbolising and suggesting a form or shape without trying to make an exact copy. The initial challenge was to find a way of representing the Museum's distinctive spiral gallery. Once the artist discovered a way to do this using dishes and other LEGO bricks, the key challenge was to make the rest of the model work at the same scale. Adam Reed Tucker achieved this via more than 20 different versions of the model, gradually arriving at a final version in which the proportions harmonised. The original Museum designed by Wright was integrated with the backdrop of the office building, as envisioned inthe original drawings. The spiral gallery, the curving facade on 5th Avenue and the entrance are all there. The result is a model that is instantly recognisable.

The bright, curved museum stands out in Manhattan.

**Building** Solomon R. Guggenheim Museum®
**Architect** Frank Lloyd Wright
**Location** New York City, New York, U.S.A.
**Building type** Art Museum

**Year** 1943-1959
**Construction type** Reinforced poured concrete
**Height** 28 m
**Square footage** 51,000 sq. ft
**Architecture style** Modernist

*"This was probably the trickiest of all the buildings in the series to interpret in LEGO bricks. The key is that the model is a representation, not an exact replication."*

**Adam Reed Tucker**

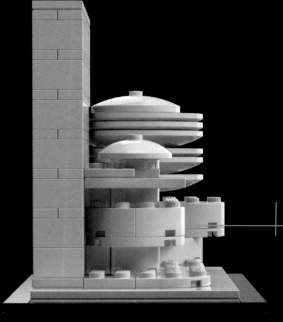

Curved bricks
represent the
Museum's famous
facade on New York
City's 5th Avenue.

The dishes of the "drum"
abut properly through
a notch in the annexe,
representing the close
harmony of the two
definitive buildings.

The annexe is built using
alternating rows of bricks
and plates. This creates
a surface texture of lines
where the pieces join that
is reminiscent of the outer
walls of the actual building
with its rhythm of verticals
and horizontals.

A series of six dishes,
arranged in groups of
three, two and one, define
the gallery "drum", with its
deep top section and
shallower lower levels.

# THE MODEL

In order to model the entire Guggenheim
Museum in approximately 200 LEGO bricks,
the artist simplified the design of the
building. With this minimalist approach, the
focus was to concentrate on the structure's
key features – the gallery "drum", the smaller
tower to the left, the curving frontage and
the annexe building. The challenge was
capturing their relative positions and
proportions, without overloading the
compact model with detail. Although in
reality the Museum is clad with very pale
beige stucco, the model uses mainly white
bricks – which look slightly darker in artificial
light – to reflect the model's minimalism.

## Model 21004

The image on the packaging shows how the iconic Museum structure stands out against the simplicity of the building behind it.

**LEGO artist** Adam Reed Tucker
**LEGO builder** Steen Sig Andersen
**LEGO bricks** 203
**Building steps** 34
**Dimensions** 143 x 102 mm
**Release date** 2009

**LEGO Architecture**

Solomon R. Guggenheim Museum®
New York City, New York, USA

10+
21004
Architect Series
Architect Series
Serie Architecture
Serie Arquitectónica
Serie Arquitectos
Építész sorozat

designed by
Adam Reed Tucker

The dark base provides a visual frame for the model, a physical foundation for its construction and a space for the label.

Immediately above the model's base, curving plates evoke low walls. The space between them represents the entrance into the Museum.

# IN FOCUS

The model is built up in layers on a base of black plates, on top of which white tiles mirror the sidewalk and the central pathway to the building's entrance doors. Adam Reed Tucker found an unconventional solution to the problem of constructing the "drum". The structure's form demanded that the dishes be placed with their studs facing downwards. To give them stability, a LEGO® Technic axle, placed in a 2x2 round brick with an axle hole, provides a central spine. Round plates act as spacers between the groups of dishes, to create the impression of the gaps between the different levels of Frank Lloyd Wright's great spiral.

A row of tiles gives a smooth finish to the flat roof of the annexe.

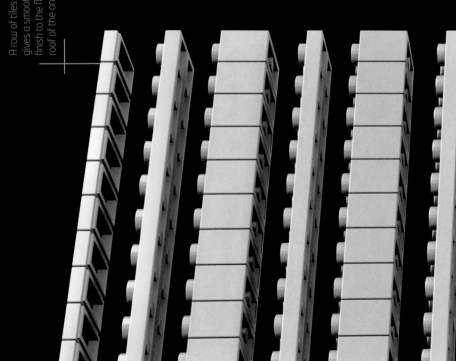

A small dish represents the domed roof.

Dishes are arranged with their studs facing downwards.

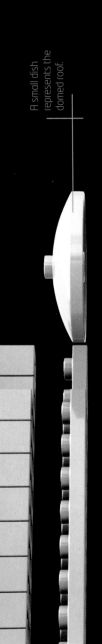

A notch in the structure of the annexe allows the main building to fit against it snugly.

4x4 round plate faces downwards.

A jumper plate enables the annexe to be offset slightly, so that it is closely integrated with the main building.

A LEGO Technic axle provides central support for the dishes.

Tiles represent the square walls immediately beneath the small dome.

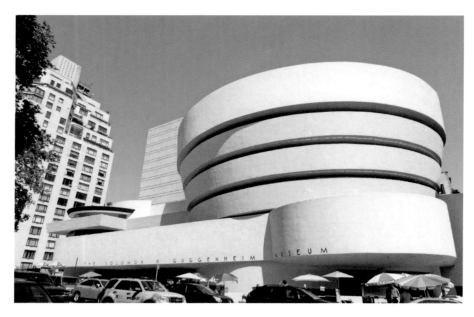

**The Rotunda**
The rotunda encases a spiral ramp with spaces where works of art are displayed. It circumscribes the main gallery. Above is a huge glazed dome that floods the central atrium with light.

# THE ORIGINAL

When Wright took on the commission to design the Guggenheim Museum in 1943, he had no idea that it would be 15 years before the building was completed. During that long gestation period the design changed substantially. Wright had to alter his plans to fit in with New York City's building codes, and also made many fine adjustments, including changes to the angle of the main gallery walls to create more effective lighting. The functions of some of the spaces also changed – the left-hand part of the building, originally intended to house apartments for Guggenheim and his curator, Hella Rebay, was eventually used for offices, workrooms and other museum functions. Throughout all these changes however, Wright's

big idea remained intact – the inverted truncated "drum" containing the spiral ramp of the main gallery. This was designed so that visitors would take the elevator to the top floor, then walk down the gently sloping ramp viewing the works of art; a way of reducing the fatigue associated with museum-visiting. The architect also saw the spiral as an "organic" form, in clear contrast to the straight-walled architecture of New York. Since it opened in 1959, not long after Wright's death, the Museum has been celebrated as one of the greatest examples of Wright's organic architecture and one of the most iconic Museum buildings in the world.

**Icon on 5th Avenue**
The Museum has been described as a symphony of curves. The main impression of the building is of its sweeping main facade with the elegantly spaced lettering and large inverted "drum" of the main gallery above. Other, smaller elements, such as the low walls at ground level that seem to invite the pedestrian into the building, also have a curving form. A combination of rounded elements, the way the "drum" expands as it rises and the pale render covering the building, make the Museum distinctive and in complete contrast to the rectilinear structures that surround it.

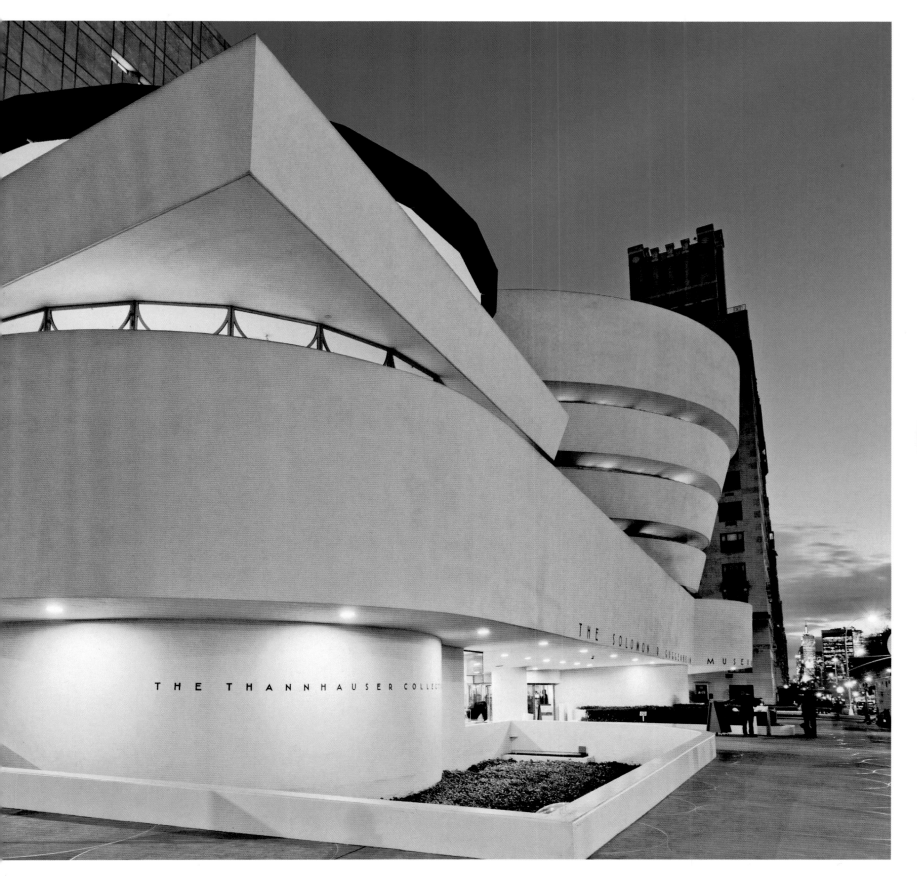

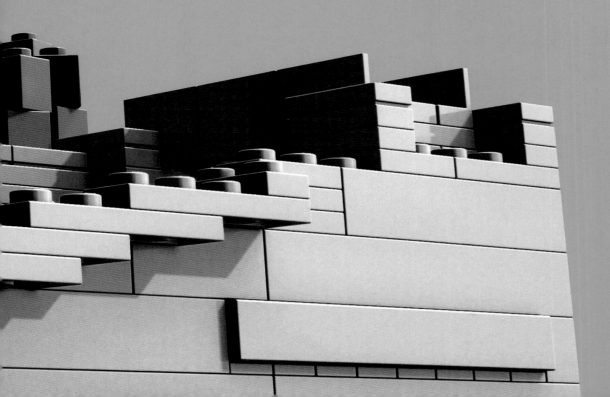

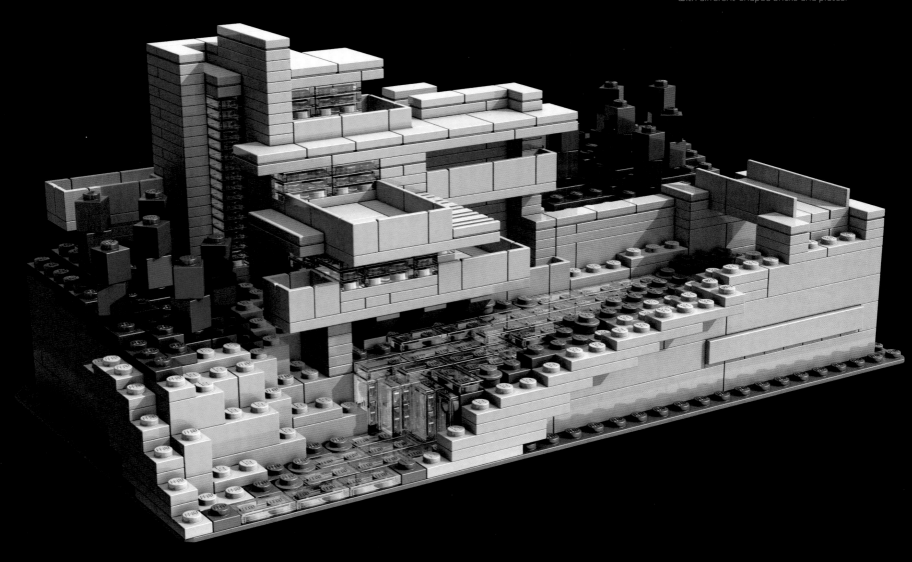

## An Organic Design

The house stands strongly against the dark green trees on either side of the model. The building spreads out horizontally, with terraces reaching over the water and into the foliage while the path and bridge take the structure further into the landscape to the right. Adam Reed Tucker chose to use bricks of the same colour for both the concrete and stone parts of the building, because a different colour adjacent to the beige and transparent bricks would have made the model too confused and visually cluttered. The differences in material are instead brought out with different-shaped bricks and plates.

# FALLINGWATER®

## LEGO® Artist: Adam Reed Tucker

Perched above a waterfall in the Pennsylvania highlands, Fallingwater is remarkable for its setting, its design and above all the way the two integrate, making it seem as if the house is part of the bedrock beneath. Showing this integration between house and environment, and interpreting the trees, rocks and water of the site using the medium of LEGO® bricks was one of the major challenges that came with designing the model. Aware that it is impossible to reproduce trees and rocks literally using plastic bricks, Adam Reed Tucker tried an abstract approach during the development process of the model, making a large version in which grey poles represented the trees. The finished version is a compromise between abstract and realistic, using green bricks for the foliage and round brown plates for the tree trunks, but arranging them in a semi-abstract, almost cubist way. The stream and waterfall show a similar approach, using transparent bricks and tiles.

The model recreates the building's mix of overhanging horizontals – the terraces and flat roofs of concrete – and soaring vertical elements built of stone, the whole thing resting, like the original building itself, on massive piers that look like huge inverted buttresses. The finished model looks impressive, but its interest goes much deeper than the surface – it is designed so that it can be slid and lifted apart, allowing glimpses into the interior and insights into the structure.

Fallingwater is angular but nestles into the landscape perfectly.

**Building** Fallingwater®
**Architect** Frank Lloyd Wright
**Location** Mill Run, Pennsylvania, U.S.A.
**Building type** Residential house
**Year** 1935–1937
**Construction type** Reinforced concrete plus sandstone
**Height** 28 m
**Square footage** 2,885 sq. ft
**Architecture style** Modernist

*"I wanted to engage the builder and to make the model interactive and dynamic. It slides apart sequentially, like a Japanese puzzle box".*

**Adam Reed Tucker**

# THE MODEL

Much of the masonry of the house is represented by LEGO bricks that have a thin profile, especially plates, tiles and angled plates. This helps to emphasise the spreading, horizontal nature of the building, a feature that it has in common with many of Frank Lloyd Wright's other house designs. The model contrasts this spreading quality of the building with the large, solid-looking bricks that make up the underlying bedrock, while using the same colour bricks for both stone and concrete emphasises the way in which the house is at one with its setting, a true example of Frank Lloyd Wright's organic architecture.

Transparent plates provide a way of portraying the large windows, which are made up of numerous shallow panes in the real house.

Using different-sized plates for these stone parts of the house gives a surface texture similar to the thin blocks of stone used in the original building.

Angled plates make up the low walls that surround all of the terraces on the model.

Brown circular plates represent the tree trunks.

Large bricks depict the massive natural stones on which the house stands.

## Model 21005

A sizeable and complex model, Fallingwater uses its large number of bricks to represent both the house and its surroundings.

**LEGO artist** Adam Reed Tucker
**LEGO builder** Steen Sig Andersen
**LEGO bricks** 811
**Building steps** 37
**Dimensions** 256 x 117 mm
**Release date** 2009

**LEGO** Architecture

Fallingwater®
Mill Run, Pennsylvania

Ages
16+
21005
Cont **811** pcs
Construction model
Architect series
1st edition
designed by
Adam Reed Tucker
Building Toy

Book included
with details on
design and history

Green 1x1 bricks are positioned at an angle to symbolise the organic nature of the trees' foliage.

The trellis over the terrace is represented by a series of grilles with narrow bars.

As well as providing access, the bridge also helps link the house visually to the landscape.

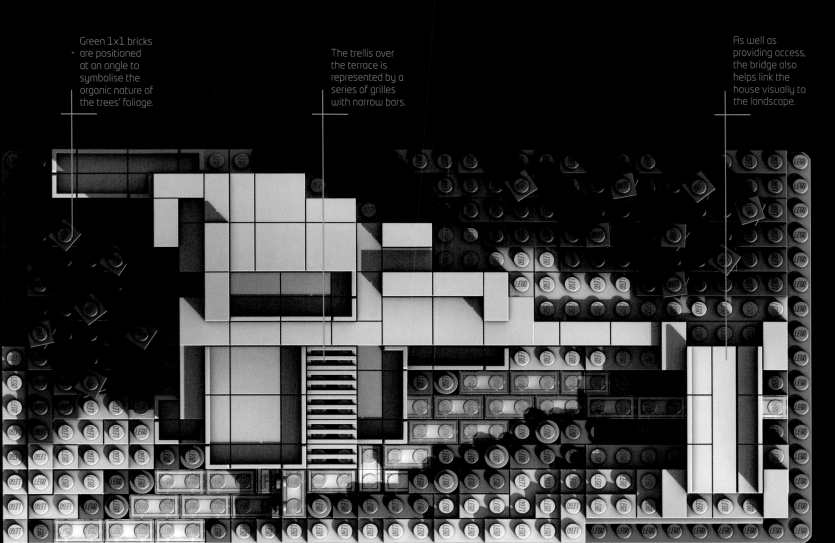

# IN FOCUS

At the time of its creation, Fallingwater was the largest model in the LEGO Architecture series, and Adam Reed Tucker wanted to make it involving to build and to include an interactive element. Taking his inspiration from Japanese puzzle boxes, the artist created a model in which the separate elements interlock and slide apart, mirroring the dynamic design of the house itself. The roof, the house's different levels and even the base can be removed, revealing the inner parts and structure of the building. To achieve this, and still keep the model faithful to the design of the original house, the elements had to be perfectly balanced and precisely designed.

The flat roof of the third level is constructed of two layers of tiles.

The third level is attached to the flat roof of tiles that covers the level beneath.

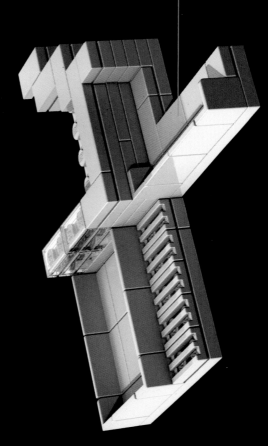

A trellis, formed of grilles, shading terrace beneath.

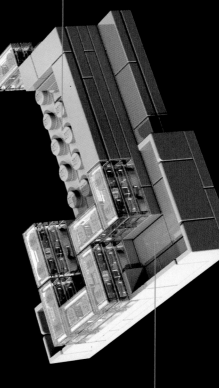

The second level has a large terrace.

The main level with windows made of transparent bricks slides out from the structure below.

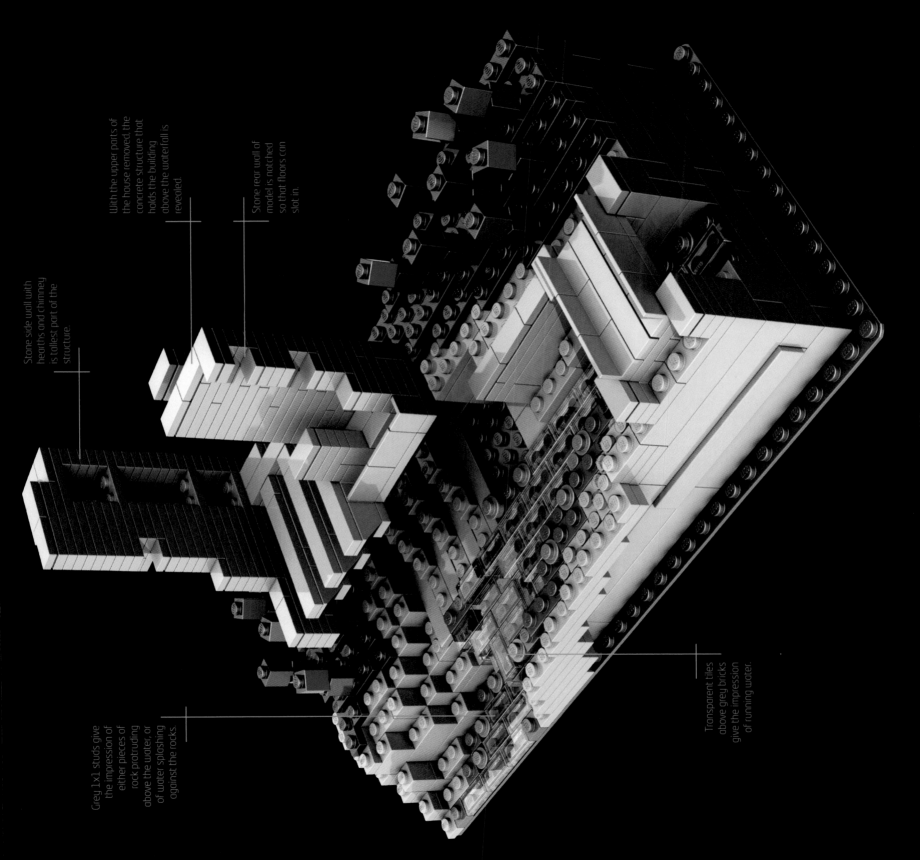

Stone side wall with hearths and chimney is tallest part of the structure.

With the upper parts of the house removed, the concrete structure that holds the building above the waterfall is revealed.

Stone rear wall of model is notched so that floors can slot in.

Grey 1x1 studs give the impression of either pieces of rock protruding above the water, or of water splashing against the rocks.

Transparent tiles above grey bricks give the impression of running water.

**Organic Living Space**
In the spacious main living room, the floor is paved with stone and near the hearth the natural rocks beneath the building protrude upwards through the floor. This shows the close bond between building and site that is one of the features of Frank Lloyd Wright's organic architecture. Long windows look out towards the trees and admit plenty of natural light.

# THE ORIGINAL

Frank Lloyd Wright designed Fallingwater as a weekend house for Pittsburgh department store owner Edgar J. Kaufmann. Kaufmann wanted a house near the waterfall of his mountain acreage. Wright chose to build along the streambed and cantilever the house over the rocks and waterfall. Inside is a large living room on the main level, with stairs directly down to the water below. Bedrooms and bathrooms are on the two levels above, and every level has generous terraces – in several cases larger than the rooms they adjoin. Most rooms also have large windows, and these have slender glazing bars so that the views out are broad and uninterrupted. The materials, including local sandstone and North Carolina black walnut, are used unadorned so that their natural surface qualities can be enjoyed. The result is a building of great dynamism.

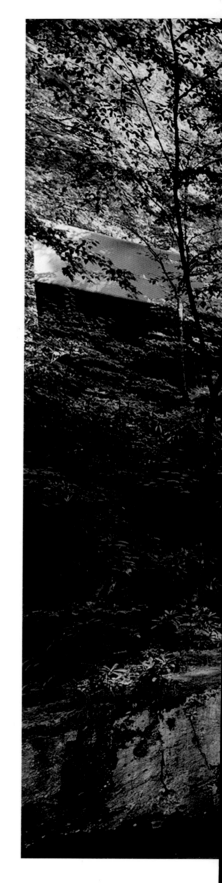

**Reaching Out to the Landscape**
Trees, rocks and water dominate Fallingwater's rural Pennsylvania site. While the stone-built portions of the house seem grounded and integrated with the natural stone beneath, the cantilevered terraces seem to float free in the landscape, almost touching the surrounding dense foliage. Beneath, a shadow conceals the house's supporting masonry above the constant stream of the waterfall, which catches the light.

# THE WHITE HOUSE

## House and Setting

Almost everyone who has seen the White House, in person or through the media, knows it is surrounded by its famous gardens and when producing the model, Adam Reed Tucker was also conscious of the building's environment. By using a green base and including some semi-abstract trees to frame the white structure, the model reminds us of all the images we have seen of the house surrounded by its lawns and shrubs, helping us to recreate both the building and its setting in the mind's eye.

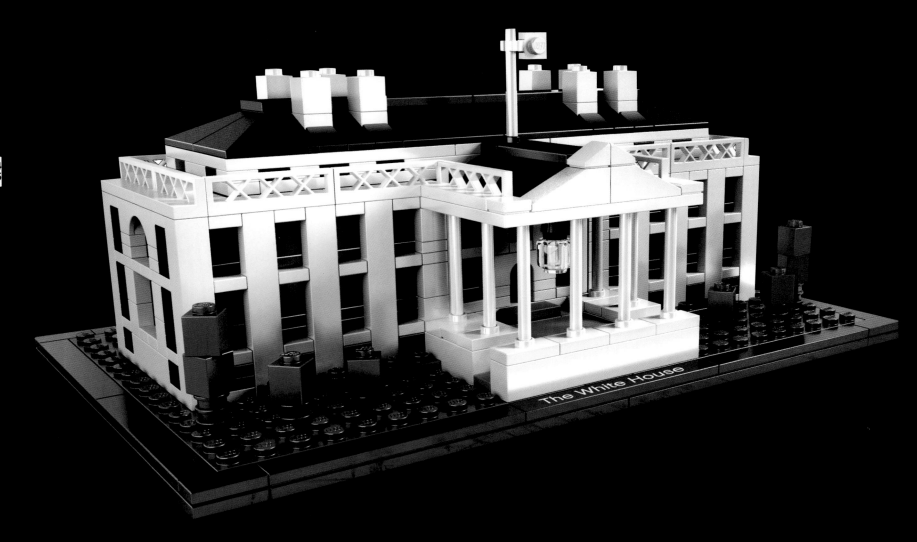

The White House

# THE WHITE HOUSE

## LEGO® Artist: Adam Reed Tucker

One of the most recognisable buildings in the world, and a symbol of the USA and its President, the White House was an obvious candidate for the LEGO® Architecture series. Adam Reed Tucker chose to concentrate on the main, central part of the building. This is the original White House, designed by James Hoban in the neoclassical style and built in the 1790s, which still includes the state rooms and presidential apartments. The East and West Wings, which contain offices, are not included in the model.

While in many ways the model is very close to the original – for example, there are the correct numbers of windows on the main facades and the right number of columns on the north front's portico – the scale did not allow the small classical details of the White House to be reproduced. By concentrating on the proportions, and by introducing subtle adjustments in the construction of details such as the windows and parapets, the artist produced a model that is a recreation of the original in the medium of LEGO bricks.

The White House's grounds are very recognisable.

**Building** The White House
**Architect** James Hoban
**Location** Washington D.C., USA
**Building type** Presidential residence

**Year** 1792–1800
**Construction type** Stone solid walls
**Square footage** 55,000 sq. ft
**Architecture style** Neoclassical

*"To represent the garden setting of the White House, I included trees built in a semi-abstract fashion, like those in the model of Fallingwater".*

**Adam Reed Tucker**

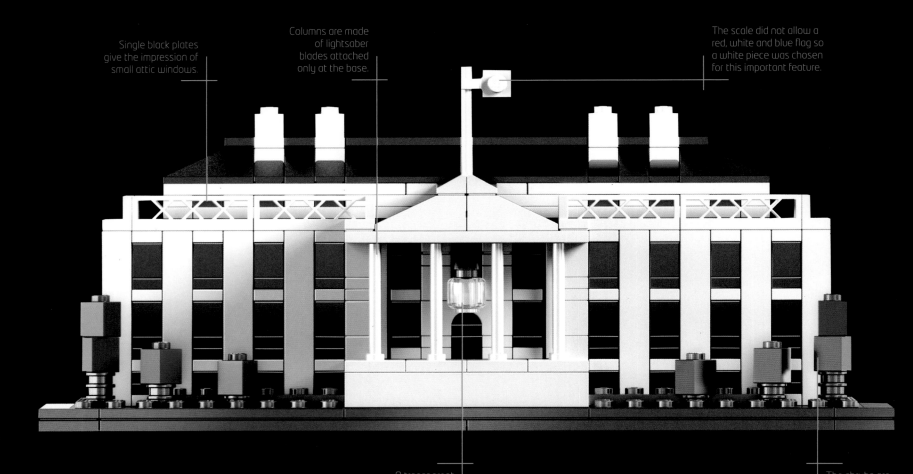

Single black plates give the impression of small attic windows.

Columns are made of lightsaber blades attached only at the base.

The scale did not allow a red, white and blue flag so a white piece was chosen for this important feature.

A transparent mini-figure head represents the pendant light fitting under the portico.

The shrubs are made of 1x1 bricks and round plates.

# THE MODEL

The main features of the White House are its white-painted stone walls, rows of regularly spaced windows and the centrepieces of its main facades – the straight-sided classical portico to the north and the curving one to the south. While the walls were straightforward to create in white LEGO bricks and plates, it would have been easy to produce the effect of a flat-sided white box. Artist Adam Reed Tucker avoided this by recessing the windows slightly, to produce shadows. The resulting pattern of light and dark, which is enhanced by the dark slopes of the building's roof, sets off the porticos and other details effectively.

Lattices create the effect of the building's baluster parapet.

## Model 21006

The finished model recreates all the key elements of the White House – including windows, porticos, parapets and chimneys – in just 560 LEGO bricks.

**LEGO artist** Adam Reed Tucker
**LEGO builder** Steen Sig Andersen
**LEGO bricks** 560
**Building steps** 34
**Dimensions** 224 x 100 mm
**Release date** 2010

**LEGO** Architecture

The White House
Washington, D.C. USA

12+
21006

Architect Series
Architect Series
Série Architecture
Serie Architectónica
Serie Arquitectos
Építész sorozat

Model designed by
Adam Reed Tucker

The black bricks that represent the windows are recessed by half a stud, to create the impression of a frame.

The columns are made of bars attached at the top to elements with horizontal clips.

Curved plates make up the balcony on the upper floor of the portico.

Black slopes represent the building's low-pitched roof.

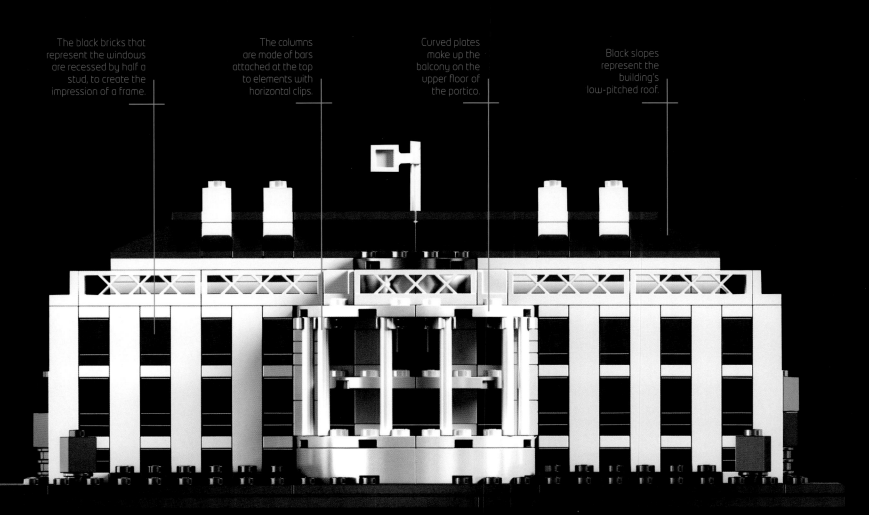

# IN FOCUS

To make the White House model look really white, the artist used tall 1x1x4 white bricks for the masonry between the windows on the north and south fronts. As well as providing structural strength, these bricks eliminate the horizontal joins that would have been present if smaller elements had been used, so that the model's walls give an impression of smooth, uninterrupted whiteness that is true to the original building. The black elements that make up the windows, by contrast, include tiles, with the joins between them suggesting the windows' glazing bars.

The chimneys of the White House are made of 1x1 white bricks.

White elements represent the top of the attic story and provide strength for the roof structure.

The parapet is made of angle lattice elements, arranged with the plates pointing outwards at each end of the building, so that the lattices join cleanly at the corners.

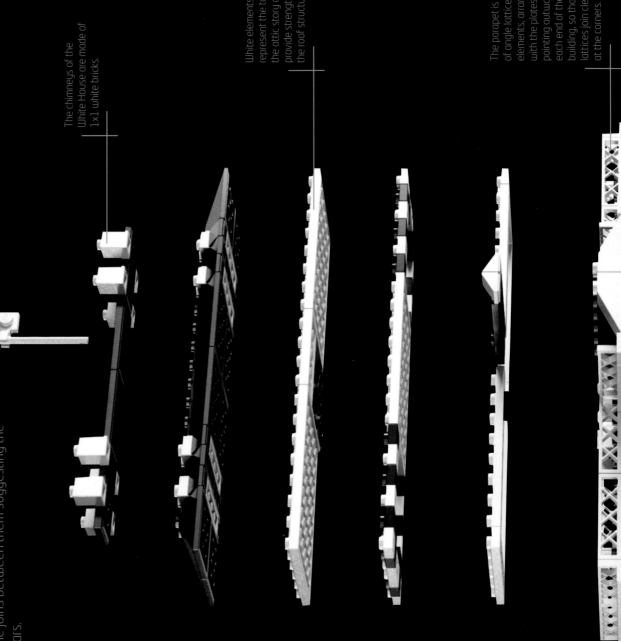

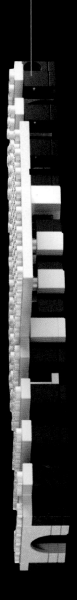

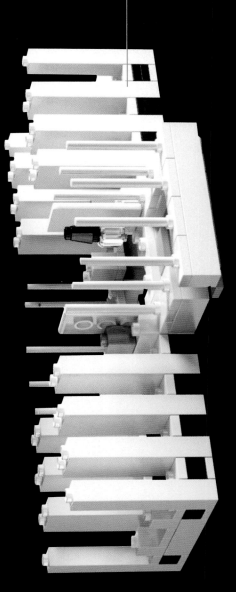

Jumper plates
allow the
windows to be
recessed between
the white bricks.

A 1x3 arch
represents the
doorway inside
the portico.

Tall 1x2x5 white
bricks make up the
masonry between
the main windows.

**The South Portico**
Hoban added the portico in 1830. This semicircular feature matches the neoclassical style of the building, but breaks its geometry of straight lines in a pleasing way. Hoban may have modelled it on the portico of the Château de Rastignac.

**James Hoban**
(c.1758–1831)
Hoban studied drawing in Dublin and moved to North America in the 1780s. Having begun his architectural practice in Philadelphia, Hoban became known for imposing buildings in the neoclassical style, such as the County Courthouse at Charleston, South Carolina, and was also one of the architects who worked on the Capitol.

# THE ORIGINAL

In 1792 a competition was held for designs for the new Presidential residence in Washington, D.C. President George Washington selected a design by the architect James Hoban as the winner. Hoban's design in the neoclassical style, with its round columns, triangular pediment and rows of equally spaced windows was in keeping with similar buildings being constructed in North America. The President asked Hoban to modify his design slightly, widening the main facades, and concealing the ground floor behind a carriage ramp to create the main part of the building that we see today and that is the one recreated in the LEGO model.

The house was virtually destroyed by fire during the War of 1812 and was rebuilt along the same lines as the original. In the years after the rebuilding, the classical porticos were added. The resulting house featured high-quality decoration, including some of the finest architectural carving of the period, but balanced this with the extensive plain white wall surfaces that gave the building its name and helped to create the distinctive building that is so familiar today. The 20th century saw numerous restorations to the existing structure, and the addition of the East and West Wings.

**The North Face**
Floodlit at night, the north side of the White House, with its portico and triangular pediment, is a beautiful example of classical symmetry. In designing it, James Hoban was influenced both by the neoclassical buildings he had seen in Europe and by structures in the classical colonial style fashionable in North America at the time.

# FARNSWORTH HOUSE™

## Suspended Above the Ground

The model elegantly portrays the way in which the house and its adjoining terrace are set on their supports slightly above the level of the surrounding grass in the original house's rural setting. The floor and roof slabs, each constructed with two layers of LEGO plates and tiles, cantilever out from their supports, as in the actual building, to give the whole structure a sense of weightlessness. In a similar way, the steps seem to have only minimal supports, reducing their apparent connection with the underlying ground.

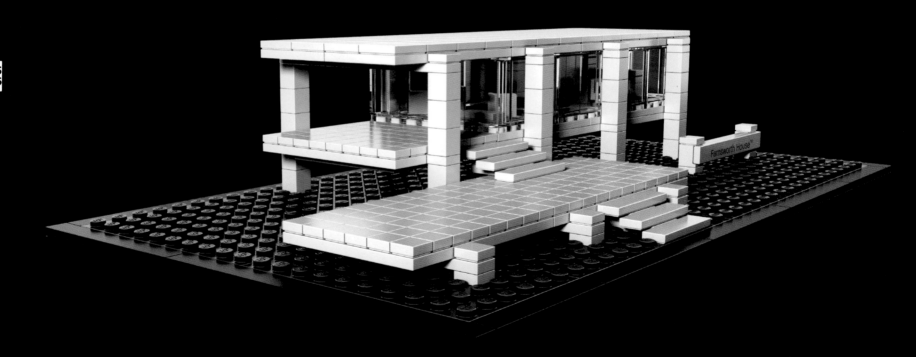

# FARNSWORTH HOUSE™

**LEGO® Artist: Adam Reed Tucker**

The Farnsworth House, designed by modernist master Ludwig Mies van der Rohe, is the ultimate in minimalism, with a single living space, walls made completely of glass and a structure that seems to float above the surrounding grass in Plano, Illinois. A design of such simplicity was a huge challenge for LEGO® artist Adam Reed Tucker, for whom the main issue was getting the proportions right and recreating the way in which the glass box is suspended between its slender vertical supports. White LEGO bricks and plates were the obvious elements for the main structure of the building, together with the terrace and entrance steps that form such an important part of the exterior.

An unusual aspect of this model is the importance of the building's interior. Because the glass walls put the inside of the building on display, the house is as much about its furnishings and fittings as it is about the meticulous proportions of the structure. The model therefore includes a central core unit to represent the wooden structure containing the kitchen and bathrooms, as well as adding small but carefully modelled representations of the furniture. Always aiming for simplicity, these interior details reflect the minimalist spirit of this famous house.

The overhanging roof of the house provides a generous open-air seating area.

**Building** Farnsworth House™
**Architect** Ludwig Mies van der Rohe
**Location** Plano, Illinois, U.S.A.
**Building type** House
**Year** 1945–1951

**Construction type** Steel framework, glass walls
**Height** Approx. 6 m
**Square footage** 1,500 sq. ft
**Architecture style** Modernist

*"With its uninterrupted walls of glass, this building is all about putting the interior on display".*

**Adam Reed Tucker**

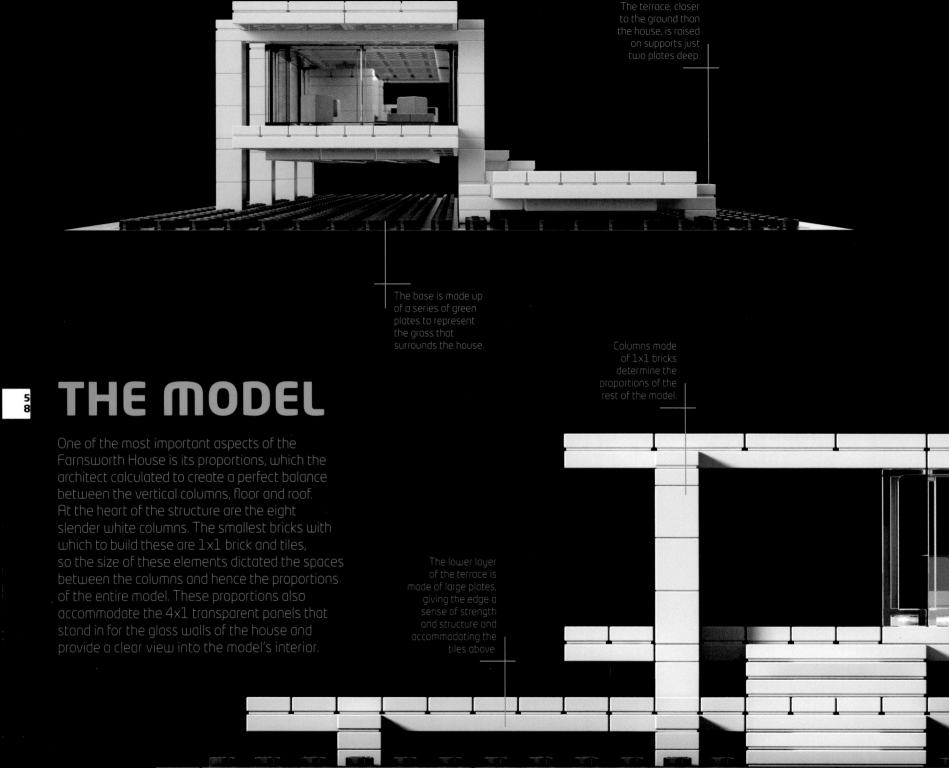

The terrace, closer to the ground than the house, is raised on supports just two plates deep.

The base is made up of a series of green plates to represent the grass that surrounds the house.

Columns made of 1x1 bricks determine the proportions of the rest of the model.

The lower layer of the terrace is made of large plates, giving the edge a sense of strength and structure and accommodating the tiles above.

5
8

# THE MODEL

One of the most important aspects of the Farnsworth House is its proportions, which the architect calculated to create a perfect balance between the vertical columns, floor and roof. At the heart of the structure are the eight slender white columns. The smallest bricks with which to build these are 1x1 brick and tiles, so the size of these elements dictated the spaces between the columns and hence the proportions of the entire model. These proportions also accommodate the 4x1 transparent panels that stand in for the glass walls of the house and provide a clear view into the model's interior.

## Model 21009

A set comprising more than 540 LEGO bricks produces a faithful model of the Farnsworth House that stands out in white against the green of the base plates.

**LEGO artist** Adam Reed Tucker
**LEGO builder** Steen Sig Andersen
**LEGO bricks** 546
**Building steps** 34
**Dimensions** 304 x 66 mm
**Release date** 2011

LEGO Architecture

Farnsworth House™
Plano, Illinois, USA

12+
21009

Architect Series
Architect Series
Serie Arquitectónica
Série Architectes
Építész sorozat
Série Arquitectos

Model designed by
Adam Reed Tucker

To represent Mies's unobstructed glass walls, the artist chose window panels that would give the slightest possible sense of a join.

1x2 tiles set on their side give a sense of the proportions of the cabinets in the central unit.

Angled tiles set obliquely give the impression of swivelling chairs.

Farnsworth House™

# IN FOCUS

Looking at the model in exploded view shows how the floor and roof slabs, although very thin, are actually built in layers. This enables them to have upper surfaces of non-structural tiles (1x1 tiles for the floor, 2x2 for the roof), with lower levels of larger plates that hold the structure together and provide connection points with the uprights. Another result of this layered construction is that there is a clear division along the edges of the roof between tiles and plates, reflecting the shadow gap running along the edge of the roof slab in the actual house.

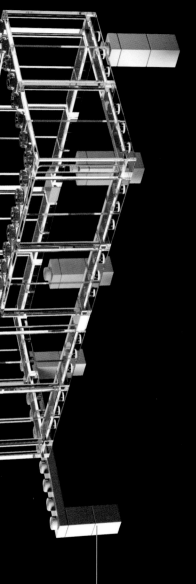

The roof is made up of plates with tiles laid on top; the tiles stand above the supporting pillars, helping to create the impression that the roof is "floating."

Brown tiles recreate the effect of wooden table tops.

The walls are made up entirely of transparent panels.

1x10 plate acts as a discreet support for the building's overhanging roof.

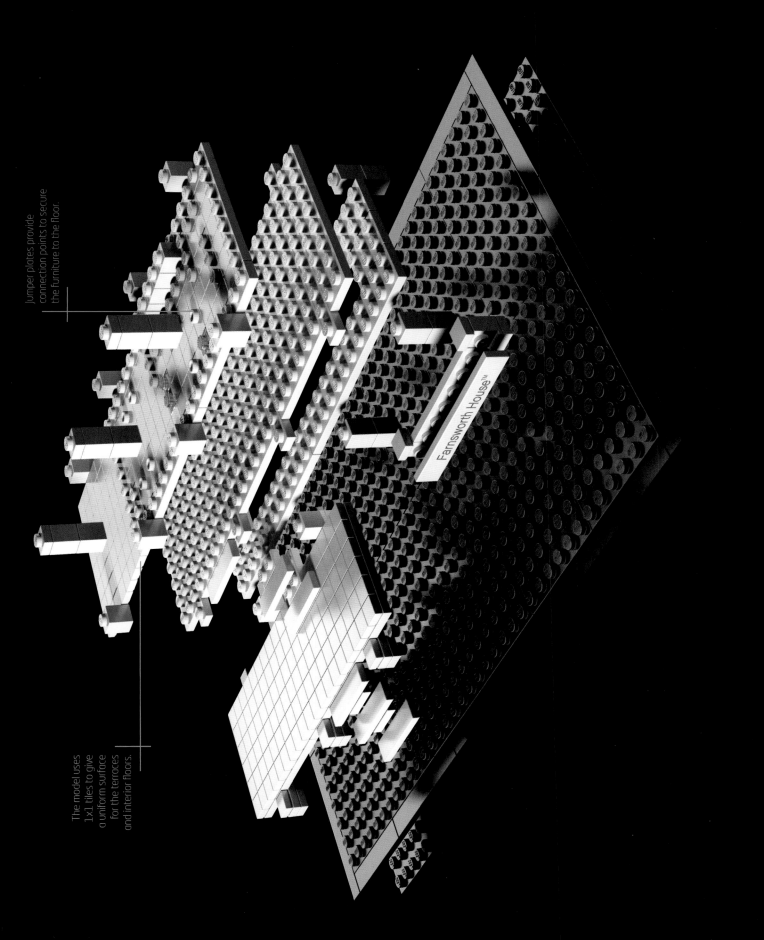

Jumper plates provide connection points to secure the furniture to the floor.

The model uses 1x1 tiles to give a uniform surface for the terraces and interior floors.

Farnsworth House™

**Ludwig Mies van der Rohe**
(1886–1969)
German-born Mies was one of the greatest pioneers of modern architecture, developing a pure, minimalist style and using modern "industrial" materials such as steel and plate glass in combination with immaculately finished surfaces. He became influential in Europe, designing the Barcelona Pavilion and becoming director of the Bauhaus, before embarking on projects in the U.S.A.

**Designer Chairs**
Furnishings include chairs that Mies designed for an earlier project, Tugendhat House. Their design echoes the sleek lines of the house.

# THE ORIGINAL

In 1945, medical practitioner Dr. Edith Farnsworth commissioned the great modernist architect Ludwig Mies van der Rohe, who was by then living in the U.S.A., to design a weekend retreat near Plano, Illinois. Mies had developed his disciplined, minimalist architecture in Europe in buildings such as the German Pavilion for the 1929 Barcelona World Exposition. The Farnsworth House, constructed in 1949–51, gave him the opportunity to take minimalism still further, reducing the house to floor and roof slabs, eight steel supporting columns and walls of glass. Apart from the wood-finished unit containing the

bathrooms and kitchen fittings, the interior is completely white, providing a perfect setting for furniture both designed by, and influenced by, Mies.

The glass walls give uninterrupted views of the exterior and allow a natural interplay with the immaculate interior. By setting the house 1.6 metres above the ground and concealing the joints between the columns and floor, Mies produced the illusion that the building's glass box was floating free.

Following flood damage the house was painstakingly restored, and it is now owned by the National Trust for Historic Preservation and is open to the public.

**Stillness in a Natural Setting**
The simple lines of the house embody perfectly the most famous saying of Mies van der Rohe: "Less is more." They create an atmosphere of stillness in contrast to the trees and grass, which move gently in the breeze. The house and setting offered the client peace and tranquility, and the opportunity to enjoy the surrounding natural beauty.

# ROCKEFELLER CENTER®

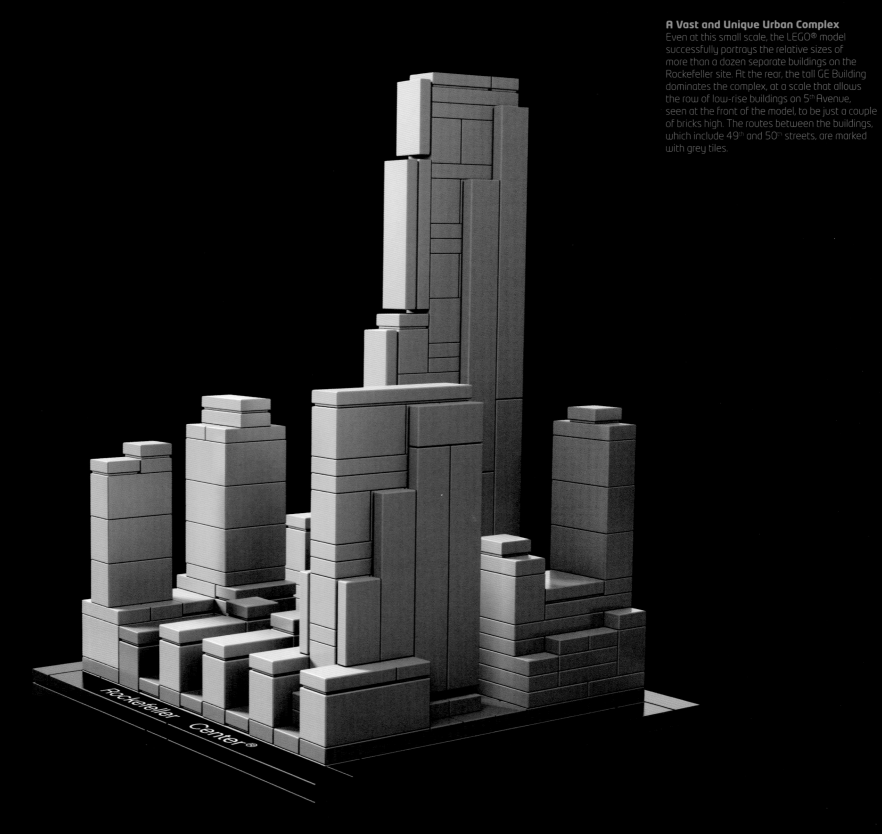

**A Vast and Unique Urban Complex**
Even at this small scale, the LEGO® model
successfully portrays the relative sizes of
more than a dozen separate buildings on the
Rockefeller site. At the rear, the tall GE Building
dominates the complex, at a scale that allows
the row of low-rise buildings on 5th Avenue,
seen at the front of the model, to be just a couple
of bricks high. The routes between the buildings,
which include 49th and 50th streets, are marked
with grey tiles.

Rockefeller Center®

# ROCKEFELLER CENTER®

**LEGO® Artist: Adam Reed Tucker**

A group of buildings between 48th and 51st streets in New York City, the Rockefeller Center was difficult to model in LEGO® bricks, especially at a small scale, because the structures range so widely in size. At the heart of the complex are the 14 original buildings, dating from the 1930s and centred on the large 70-floor GE Building, which stands behind a sunken plaza. To either side of this skyscraper are smaller, but still imposing, high-rise blocks such as the International Building, but the Rockefeller Center also includes low-rise structures such as the group facing on to 5th Avenue. To recreate these different structures, Adam Reed Tucker took his cue from the Art Deco architecture of the complex, using the SNOT (studs not on top) technique to suggest the vast surfaces and the buildings' setbacks.

The GE Building soars above the Rockefeller Center complex.

**Building** Rockefeller Center®
**Architect** Raymond Hood
**Location** New York City, U.S.A.
**Building type** Commercial development
**Year** 1930–1939

**Construction type** Steel framework faced with limestone
**Height** 258.1 m
**Square footage** Approx. 8,000,000 sq. ft
**Architecture style** Art Deco

*"The pattern of plates and tiles helps to recreate the subtle changes of relief on the facades of the buildings".*

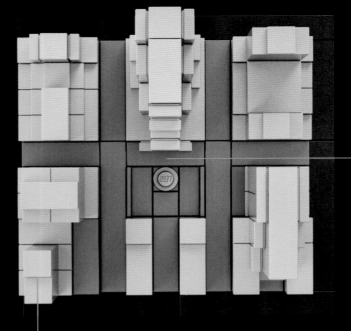

The central plaza is set one tile lower than the surrounding roads and pavements, to recreate the sunken original; a single 1x1 round tile represents its fountain.

Like several of the bricks, these buildings are linked at ground level, so they appear as one structure in the model.

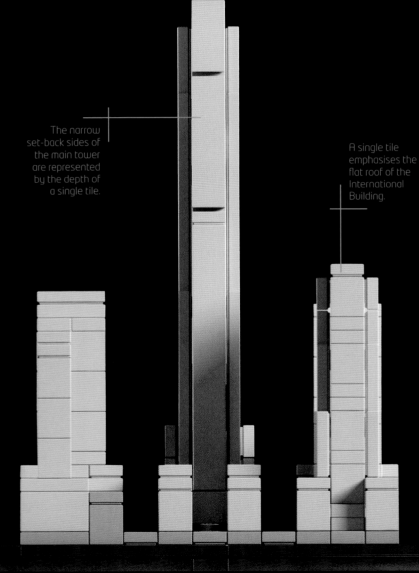

The narrow set-back sides of the main tower are represented by the depth of a single tile.

A single tile emphasises the flat roof of the International Building.

# THE MODEL

The LEGO model represents the main part of the Rockefeller Center – the area between 48th and 51st streets that contains the original 14 Art Deco buildings constructed in the 1930s and not the section on the other side of 51st street, which consists of towers added much later, in the 1960s and 1970s. These original buildings are clad in Indiana limestone, and Adam Reed Tucker decided to represent this by making almost the entire model in beige components. This uniform colour gives the model a similar visual unity to that achieved in the real buildings.

An extra tile gives
emphasis to the
principal setback
on the front of
the GE Building.

Outward-facing tiles,
with the thin joins
between them, create
the impression of the
vast vertical planes of
the building's facade.

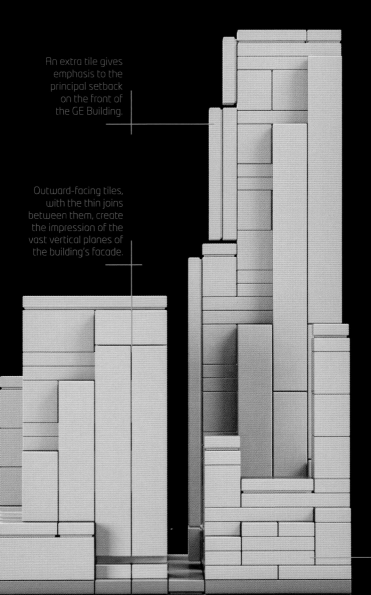

# LEGO Architecture

**Rockefeller Center®**
New York City, New York, USA

Ages
**10+**
21007
**240** pcs
Construction model
Architect series
1st edition
designed by
Adam Reed Tucker
Booklet included
with details on
design and history

## Model 21007
The finished model portrays
the 1930s complex with its
tall central tower balanced
by four shorter towers and
the line of lower buildings
producing a unified impression
on 5th Avenue.

**LEGO artist** Adam Reed
Tucker
**LEGO builder** Steen Sig
Andersen
**LEGO bricks** 240
**Building steps** 23
**Dimensions** 104 x 138 mm
**Release date** 2011

With plates and
tiles it is possible
to represent the
low wing at
the base of the
International
Building.

One of the most important features of the model's construction is the use of bricks with side studs, which form a key part of the core of several of the structures. These bricks enable tiles to be fixed vertically, with their flat surface forming the outer walls of the buildings. Using tiles in this way enabled the artist to portray the smooth planes of the Rockefeller Center's towers, while the subtle pattern of joins between tiles and bricks gives an impression of the proportions of the Art Deco exteriors. This pattern of planes and joins extends across the entire model. Only a single stud is visible – the one representing the fountain in the Rockefeller Plaza.

A plate plus a tile gives the building just enough depth at this point.

A brick with side studs on its front and sides provides fixing points for tiles on three faces of the building.

This single tile marks one of the building's main setbacks.

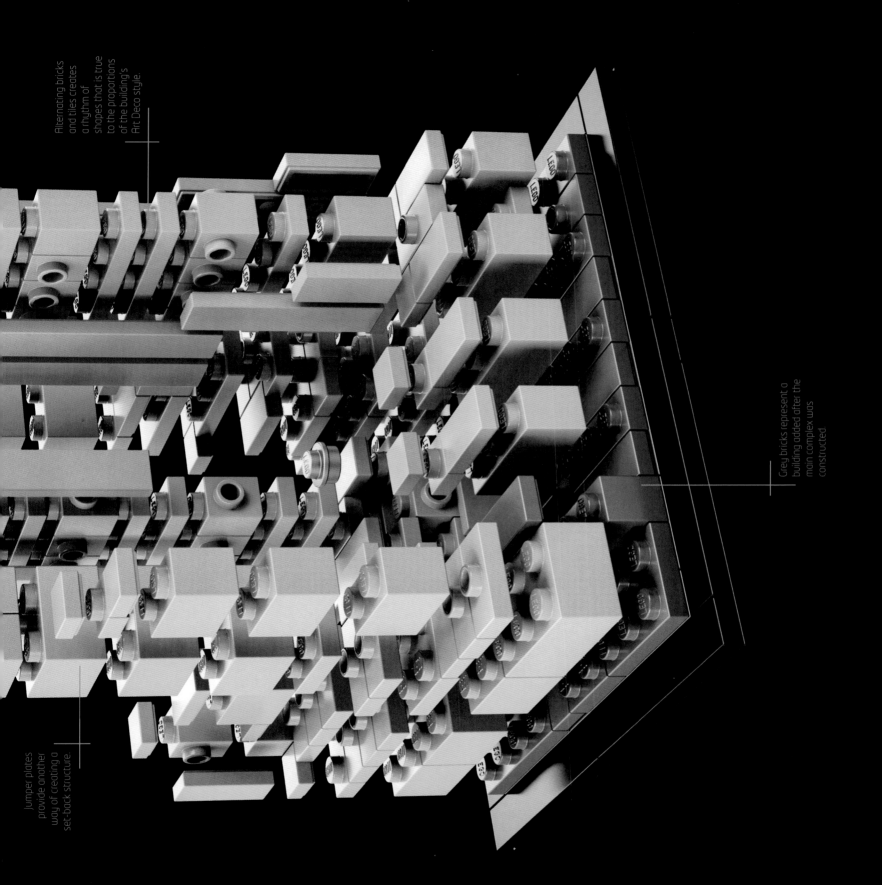

Alternating bricks and tiles creates a rhythm of shapes that is true to the proportions of the building's Art Deco style.

Grey bricks represent a building added after the main complex was constructed

Jumper plates provide another way of creating a set-back structure.

### Raymond Hood
(1881–1934)

Hood was educated at Brown University, MIT and the École des Beaux-Arts in Paris. He began as a specialist in the Gothic style, designing the huge Gothic Tribune Tower in Chicago. This led to further high-profile projects, for many of which he turned to the fashionable Art Deco style. The New York Daily News Building (1929–1930) and the McGraw Hill Building (1931) are two prominent examples in New York.

**Atlas Statue**
The bronze statue of Atlas holding the heavens by Lee Lawrie is one of the best known pieces of sculpture in the Rockefeller Center. The work was installed in 1937 and, at some 14 metres high, is a landmark on 5th Avenue.

# THE ORIGINAL

In 1928 U.S. industrialist and philanthropist John D. Rockefeller, Jr embarked on a plan to build a complex of offices and an opera house in the heart of Manhattan. After the stock market crash of 1929 made investors scarce, Rockefeller dropped the opera house from his plans and financed the whole project himself, which cost a staggering $250,000,000 over the 10-year construction period. The principal architect, Raymond Hood, planned the mix of high- and low-rise buildings which, as well office blocks, includes a large theatre, and the Radio City Music Hall. Hood designed the complex in the Art Deco

style: it features stepped setbacks and angular lines, typical of the skyscrapers of the time, but its tall blocks lack the pointed spires of most Art Deco towers.

Several of the buildings' flat tops have roof gardens and the development also features a sunken plaza that becomes a popular ice-skating rink in the winter. This concern for public space is further reflected in decorative artworks, from Paul Manship's Prometheus Fountain in the plaza to sculptures and murals on the buildings themselves. As a whole, the Rockefeller Center is one of the most striking groups of 1930s buildings ever built.

**Floodlit in Winter**
The floodlit skyscraper of the GE Building, flanked by the tall General Dynamics and International Buildings, towers above the low-rise structures of the Maison Française and British Building in front. At the foot of the GE Building is the traditional winter centrepiece of the complex, a Christmas tree that has been a feature of the site every year since 1933.

# ROBIE™ HOUSE

## A Masterpiece in Brick

The large LEGO® model clearly shows the principal elements of the house – the main block with living rooms to the left and centre, garages to the right and bedrooms and entertainment areas on the upper level, rising from the centre of the building. The whole house has a complete unity of materials, with brickwork used for the house walls, garden walls and chimneys. The model's brickwork captures the intricate pattern of right-angles created by the walls, planters, balcony, porches and garages in the original building. The red 30-degree slopes suggest the gentle pitch of the roof.

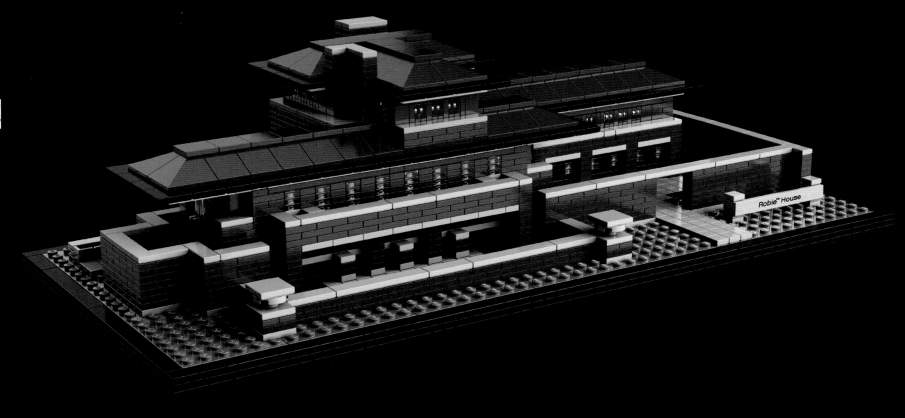

# ROBIE™ HOUSE

**LEGO® Artist: Adam Reed Tucker**

The Robie™ House in Chicago, designed by Frank Lloyd Wright, stands out because of its dramatic cantilevered roof and overhangs implemented for the porch areas creating long horizontal lines. These features, which make the house look as if it is hugging the ground, are typical of the kind of building that Wright called the "Prairie House" and they translate elegantly into this very large LEGO® model, with long plates making possible the cantilevered structure of the roof. Adam Reed Tucker made a number of key creative decisions to emphasise the horizontal character of the building. Perhaps the most important of these was the decision to make all the house walls and garden walls out of short plates. By arranging the outer wall plates in an overlapping pattern like a real brick bond, the artist represents the narrow bricks that form such a striking feature in the actual house. The model also includes rows of grey plates to recreate the concrete bases and caps of the house's walls, adding further horizontal characteristics to the structure. The result is an elegant LEGO interpretation of one of Frank

The house occupies a site in the Hyde Park neighbourhood of Chicago.

**Building** Frederick C. Robie™ House
**Architect** Frank Lloyd Wright
**Location** Chicago, Illinois, U.S.A.
**Building type** House
**Year** 1908–1910

**Construction type** Roman bricks, steel beams
**Height** 9.1 m
**Square footage** 9,062 sq. ft
**Architecture style** Modernist

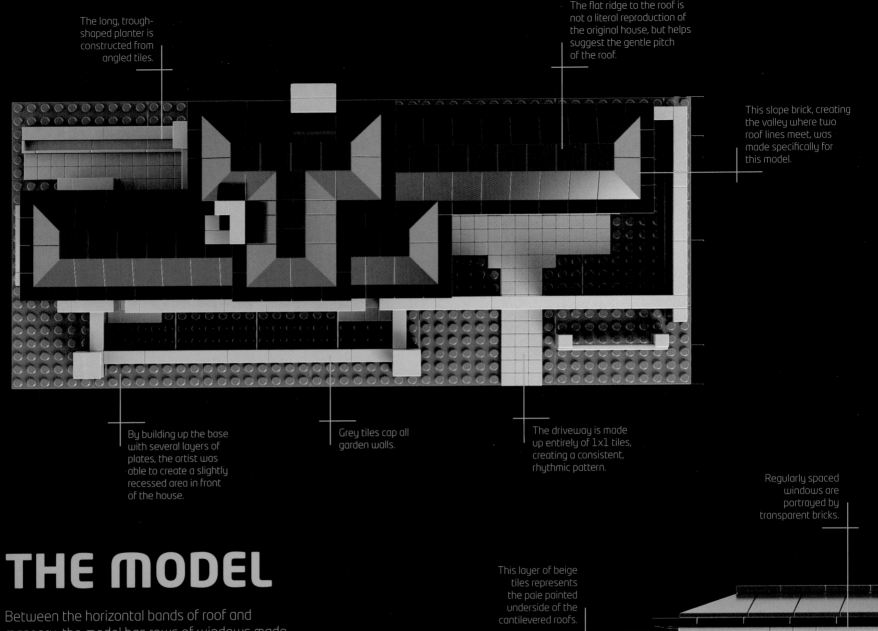

The long, trough-shaped planter is constructed from angled tiles.

The flat ridge to the roof is not a literal reproduction of the original house, but helps suggest the gentle pitch of the roof.

This slope brick, creating the valley where two roof lines meet, was made specifically for this model.

By building up the base with several layers of plates, the artist was able to create a slightly recessed area in front of the house.

Grey tiles cap all garden walls.

The driveway is made up entirely of 1x1 tiles, creating a consistent, rhythmic pattern.

# THE MODEL

Between the horizontal bands of roof and masonry, the model has rows of windows made up of transparent bricks. The sizes of these windows are carefully differentiated, with larger windows for the living rooms in the main part of the house, and smaller ones for the servants' rooms above the garages to the right. All of these windows are shaded by the generous cantilever of the roof. The artist originally intended to place LED lighting in the interior of the model so the windows could be illuminated, but this plan was abandoned. Even without the lighting, the window rows accentuate the horizontal features of the house.

Regularly spaced windows are portrayed by transparent bricks.

This layer of beige tiles represents the pale painted underside of the cantilevered roofs.

Wright's striking corner planters are recreated with a round plate and a square tile.

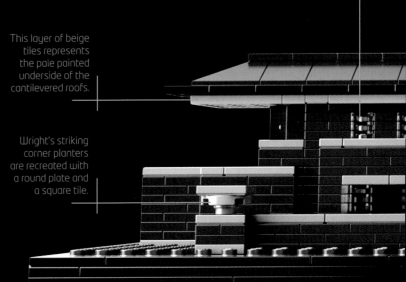

**Model 21010**
The model includes the surrounding garden walls, gateposts and similar elements, to set the Robie™ House in its immediate context.

**LEGO artist** Adam Reed Tucker
**LEGO builder** Steen Sig Andersen
**LEGO bricks** 2,276
**Building steps** 141
**Dimensions** 420 x 115 mm
**Release date** 2011

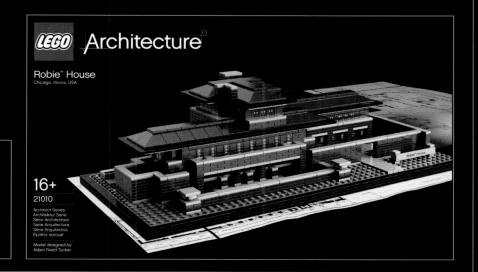

**LEGO Architecture**

Robie™ House
Chicago, Illinois, USA

16+
21010

Architect Series
Architektur Serie
Série Architecture
Serie Arquitectura
Série Arquitectos
Építész sorozat

Model designed by
Adam Reed Tucker

An ingenious use of transparent slopes set on their side allowed Adam Reed Tucker to build the house's distinctive pointed end windows.

Black bricks, contrasting with the tiles of the walls, make up the garage doors.

The layer of black tiles represents the dark guttering running around the roof; its protrusion also helps to extend the cantilevered roofline.

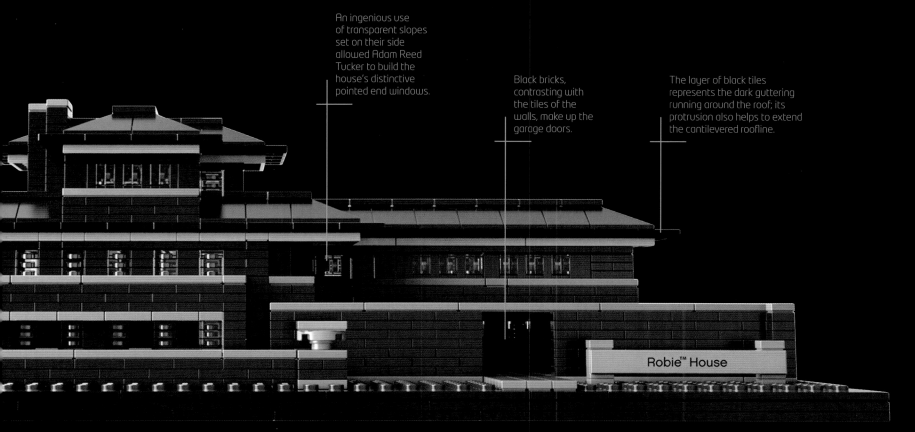

Robie™ House

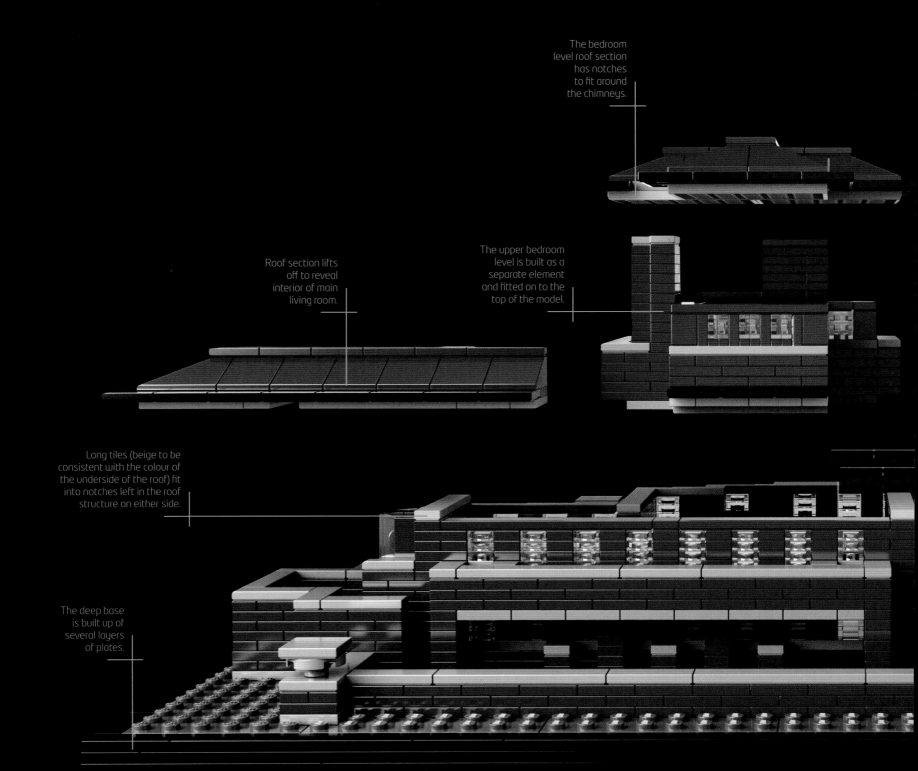

The bedroom level roof section has notches to fit around the chimneys.

Roof section lifts off to reveal interior of main living room.

The upper bedroom level is built as a separate element and fitted on to the top of the model.

Long tiles (beige to be consistent with the colour of the underside of the roof) fit into notches left in the roof structure on either side.

The deep base is built up of several layers of plates.

# IN FOCUS

This view of the model shows how the roofs and upper section of the finished building can be removed to reveal the inside. Beneath these removable parts are the main levels of the house, which are primarily built of small tiles (mainly 1x2 or 1x1). In the process of building up the walls with these tiny bricks, the builder works in a similar fashion to a bricklayer, creating the walls in layers, from the ground up. It was Adam Reed Tucker's intention that this process would help to involve the model builder closely in the construction process.

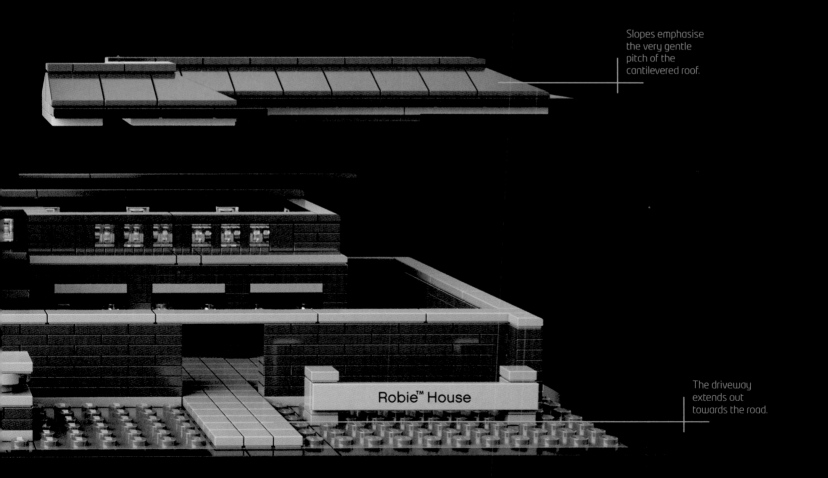

Slopes emphasise the very gentle pitch of the cantilevered roof.

Robie™ House

The driveway extends out towards the road.

**Shelter and Light: A Masterpiece of Prairie Style**
The cantilevered roofs form the strongest horizontal accents in the design, but smaller elements, such as the capstones and long, Roman-style bricks, also emphasise the horizontal lines of the house. The cantilevered roofs also have a clear practical purpose: Wright's placement of the south-facing windows serve to fill the large rooms with natural light, while the roof eliminates the strongest glare of the sun.

# THE ORIGINAL

Built for industrialist and inventor, Frederick C. Robie, Frank Lloyd Wright's Robie™ House combined both traditional and innovative construction methods and materials. Designed in 1908 and completed by 1910, the Robie™ House was one of Wright's more straightforward projects. Its structure is a mixture of conventional materials and concealed steel beams. It features Wright-designed decorative elements, such as a series of coordinated patterned art-glass windows, carpet and furniture, while introducing modern conveniences, such as a burglar alarm and industrial vacuum cleaning system.

It has a separate servants' wing featuring an airy, open-plan living room and dining room linked together by the central fireplace and stairs. Wright's vision expressed itself in the building's strong horizontal lines. The architect believed that the resulting "grounded" design of his prairie houses was beneficial, rooting the occupants to the land, whether the house was literally on the prairie, or, as here, in a city suburb. The combination of Wright's artful planning and meticulous aesthetic details have ensured that the Robie™ House is one of Wright's most successful buildings.

**Innovative art-glass windows**
At either end of the house, between the immaculately finished brickwork and the vast cantilevered roofs, two angled windows taper to a peak point, breaking the geometry of the rest of the building. Marking either end of the main house, they help bring light into the interior from the east and west, and catch the sun when it is in the south and dappled light arrives through the trees.

# BRANDENBURG GATE

### A Three-tone Gateway

The Brandenburg Gate is a sandstone structure, and the material of its walls and columns is recreated in beige LEGO® bricks, tiles and plates. Pale green elements represent the structure's roofs, and grey tiles are used for the road and pavements. This combination of shades produces an effect that is quite close to the colours of the real building. The model also portrays the proportions of the original, which has six pairs of main columns, with the gap between the central two columns slightly larger than those on either side.

# BRANDENBURG GATE

## LEGO® Artist: Adam Reed Tucker

Completed in 1791, the Brandenburg Gate stands in the centre of Berlin and is one of the most famous landmarks in Europe. At first glance it seems a simple structure of classical columns, but it poses problems for the LEGO® artist, because its columns are of two different sizes and it has a wealth of subtle classical details. Fortunately these columns are of the plainest classical order, the Doric, which has quite a simple design with uncarved square capitals at the top of each column, and this aspect of the design is not difficult to recreate using LEGO bricks. Another key area of the design is the upper part of the monument – especially the carved frieze directly above the columns, the overhanging cornice and the statue at the top, which represents a quadriga, a form of chariot drawn by four horses. All these details needed to be rendered in an abstract way to make the model work at a small scale, while authentically portraying the overall shape and arrangement of the building.

The gate's columns rise straight up from the ground, with only minimal bases.

**Building** Brandenburg Gate
**Architect** Gothard Langhans
**Location** Berlin, Germany
**Building type** Ceremonial gate
**Year** 1788-1791

**Construction type** Sandstone solid walls, columns and lintels
**Height** 19.8 m
**Square footage** 7,740 sq. ft
**Architecture style** Classic revival

*"The challenge was to recreate the proportions of the Gate, with its two different sizes of columns, while also remaining true to the monumental quality of the architecture".*

**Adam Reed Tucker**

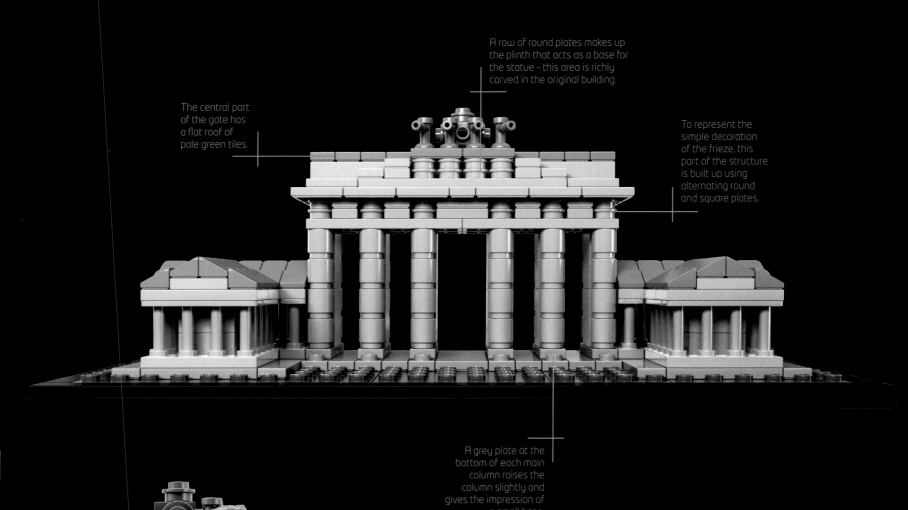

A row of round plates makes up the plinth that acts as a base for the statue – this area is richly carved in the original building.

The central part of the gate has a flat roof of pale green tiles.

To represent the simple decoration of the frieze, this part of the structure is built up using alternating round and square plates.

A grey plate at the bottom of each main column raises the column slightly and gives the impression of a small base.

The inner structure of the side pavilion, made up of 2x4 bricks, is visible through the columns.

# THE MODEL

A particular challenge for the LEGO artist was to represent the carved classical details of the Brandenburg Gate, especially in parts such as the frieze, the statue base and the statue of the four-horse chariot at the top of the gate. Adam Reed Tucker solved the problem of the frieze and statue base by using 1x1 round plates. Set next to square plates, these round bricks create slight shadows, giving the impression of decorative details carved in relief and seen from a distance. In a similar way, the artist used a number of small grey components to create the effect of the statue of the chariot.

**Model 21011**
The model uses bricks inventively to recreate the architecture of the Brandenburg Gate, while also suggesting some of the sculptural details.

**LEGO artist** Adam Reed Tucker
**LEGO builder** Steen Sig Andersen
**LEGO bricks** 363
**Building steps** 40
**Dimensions** 224 x 92 mm
**Release date** 2011

LEGO Architecture

Brandenburg Gate
Brandenburger Tor
Berlin, Germany

12+
21011

Landmark Series
Sehenswürdigkeiten
Série Monuments
Serie Monumental
Serie Edificios
Historicos
Nevezetes helyek
sorozat

Model designed by
Adam Reed Tucker

Grey bricks, originally designed as spouts for sinks, are used to represent the four horses in the statue at the top of the gate.

In the absence of a ready-made valley brick, the artist offset the two roof slopes to create the impression of the way they meet at an angle.

The pale green slopes suggest the metal-covered roofs of the original building. The Brandenburg Gate was the first LEGO model to have slopes in this colour.

# IN FOCUS

One of the most striking features of the Brandenburg Gate is that it has columns of two very different sizes – large columns, around 13 metres tall, in the middle supporting the massive transverse masonry above and smaller ones, about 7 metres tall, in the side pavilions. The artist solved the problem of representing the size difference by using round bricks for the large columns and railings for the smaller ones. Although the railings were originally designed to represent fences about one metre in height, they work well at this small scale to portray the columns of the pavilions, and even feature a slight increase in diameter top and bottom to give the effect of the column's capitals and bases.

At this scale, the artist was also able to represent the inner masonry of the structure, so that there is a sense of the walls inside the side pavilions and between the large columns of the main gate. This gives the model a strong sense of solidity, making it true to the massive original building, which was designed to be both an enduring symbol of peace between nations and a monumental tribute to the German emperor and his power.

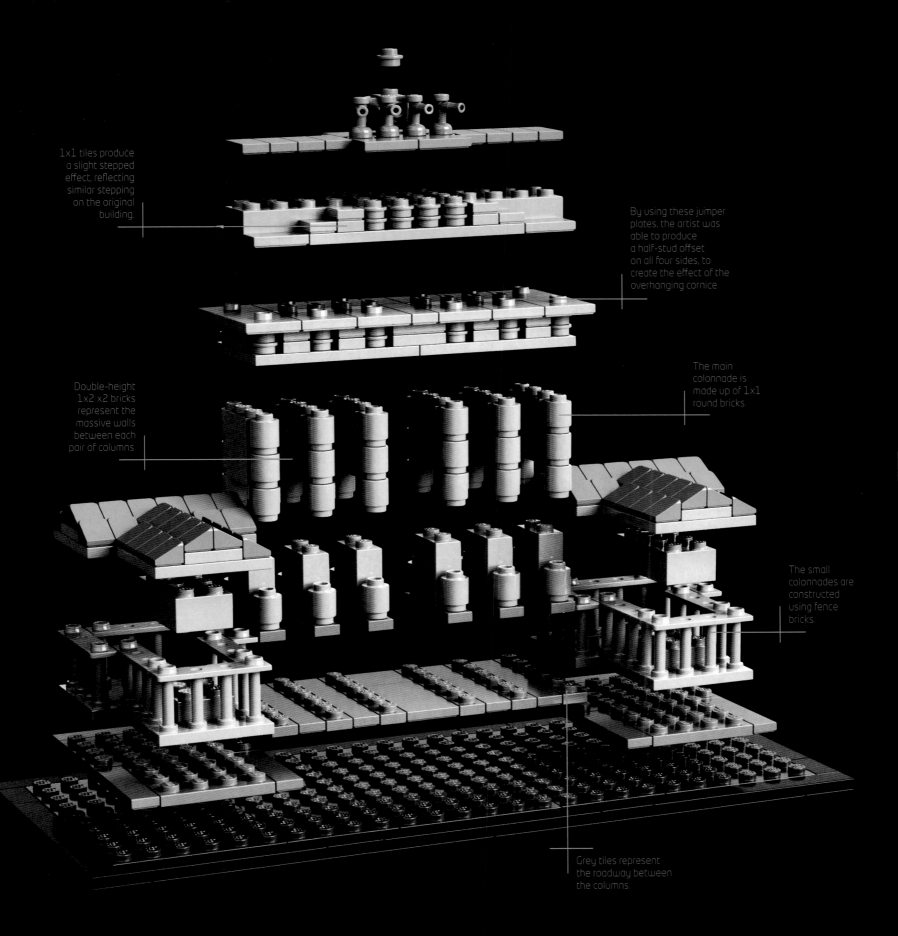

1x1 tiles produce a slight stepped effect, reflecting similar stepping on the original building.

By using these jumper plates, the artist was able to produce a half-stud offset on all four sides, to create the effect of the overhanging cornice.

The main colonnade is made up of 1x1 round bricks.

Double-height 1x2 x2 bricks represent the massive walls between each pair of columns.

The small colonnades are constructed using fence bricks.

Grey tiles represent the roadway between the columns.

### Carl Gotthard Langhans
(1732–1808)
Langhans was born in Silesia, studied law, but taught himself architecture by studying the writing of Roman architect and engineer, Vitruvius. He first worked for the Count of Hatzfeld, as a buildings inspector, and then restored palaces and constructed buildings for the Prussian royal family. He pioneered neoclassical architecture in Germany, using his fluency in the classical idiom to design his masterpiece, the Brandenburg Gate.

**The Quadriga**
The gate is crowned by a statue, by Johann Gottfried Schadow, of a quadriga driven by a female figure known either as Peace or Victory.

# THE ORIGINAL

The Brandenburg Gate was built in the 18th century at the command of the Prussian ruler Friedrich Wilhelm II to represent peace, and forms the entrance to Unter den Linden, the avenue of lime trees that led to the emperor's city palace. Langhans, the architect and court Superintendent of Buildings, designed the gate's main feature – its six pairs of tall Doric columns, forming five routes through the building, the wide central one for the imperial family and the narrower outer ones for the people of Berlin. By choosing the Greek Doric order, Langhans was following the fashion of the time for detailed buildings in an

austere classical-revival style. However, his design also had symbolic meaning because he based the gate on the Propylaea, the grand gateway to the Acropolis in Athens. By referencing the Propylaea, he was suggesting that his city was a centre of western civilisation and as important as Athens was to the ancient Greeks.

When the Berlin Wall came down in 1989, the gate became a focus for the unification of the city. As an important symbol of reunited Germany and its rich history, it was restored and was the setting for 2009's 20th anniversary celebrations of the demolition of the wall.

**The Monument's Setting**
The gate sits at the heart of Berlin, on one side of its grandest public space, the Pariser Platz, which is now mainly pedestrianised. On either side of the gate run two streets, Unter den Linden and the Strasse des 17. Juni. Just a block away from the Bundestag, or parliament building, the Brandenburg Gate reflects both the city's history and its modern importance.

# SYDNEY OPERA HOUSE™

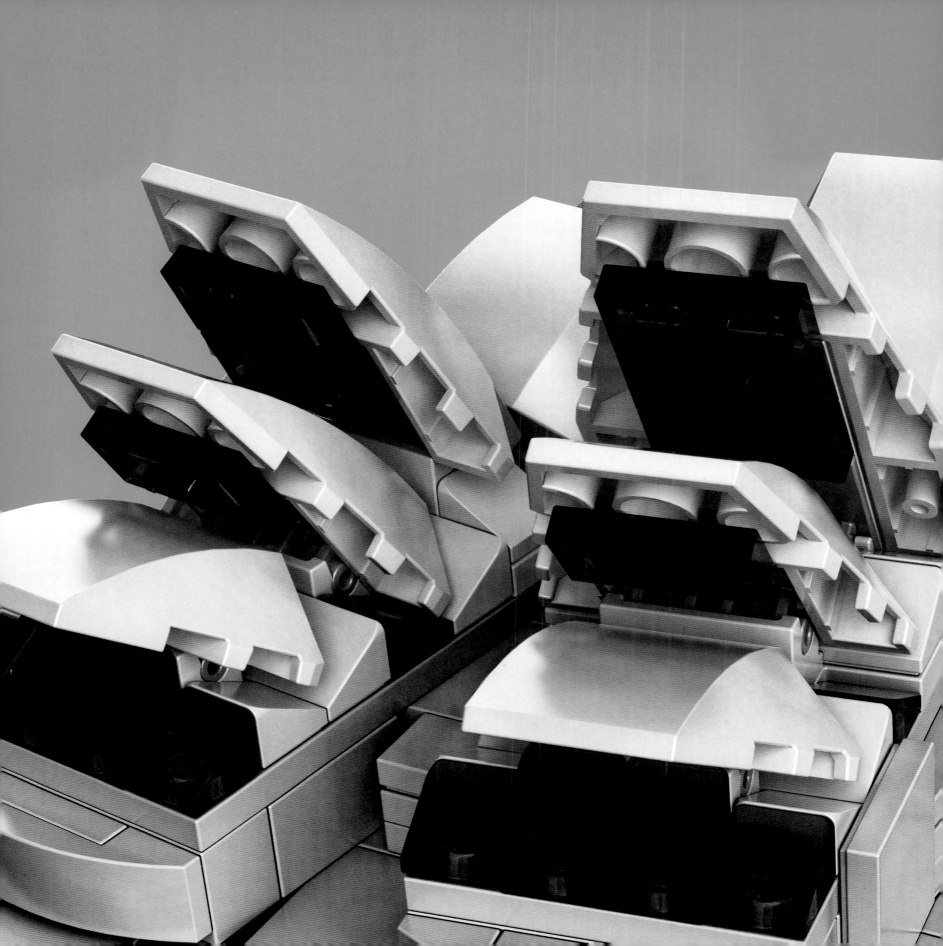

# SYDNEY OPERA HOUSE™

### LEGO® Artist: Adam Reed Tucker

The Sydney Opera House™ is Australia's most recognised building, and its stunning shape, sweeping form and perfect waterside setting have made it so famous that it has become a symbol not only of Sydney, but of the entire nation. This is thanks largely to the roof sails, but when architect Jørn Utzon first revealed his design no one knew quite how to engineer these unique structures. The sails posed a similar problem for Adam Reed Tucker when he began to design the LEGO® model of the building, because there was no LEGO brick that provided a precise match with their iconic shape. However, the artist found an approximate parallel in a type of brick with bowed and angled surfaces. These bricks are more familiar in LEGO sets featuring the *Toy Story* character Buzz Lightyear or when used to form parts of aircraft. The idea of taking them out of their context, turning them on their ends and giving them a totally new role is an example of the kind of lateral thinking that is typical of the designs in the LEGO Architecture series.

Curves and angles make up the building's distinctive shape.

**Building** Sydney Opera House™
**Architect** Jørn Utzon
**Location** Sydney, Australia
**Building type** Opera house and concert hall
**Year** 1959-1973

**Construction type** Concrete frame; ceramic roof tiles; base of reconstituted granite
**Height** 64.9 m
**Square footage** 641,292 sq. ft
**Architecture style** Modernist/expressionist

*"The key aim of the model was to capture the essence of the building, especially its unforgettable silhouette".*

**Adam Reed Tucker**

The bowed and angled bricks that make up the sails of the model are available in several sizes, so the artist could recreate the relationship between large and small shapes in the two main structures. Both the Concert Hall and Opera Theatre (Joan Sutherland Theatre) have a large shell shape in the middle, flanked by smaller ones on either side. The third structure, housing a restaurant, is topped with the smallest bricks of this type. The result is an instantly recognisable model, because it recreates the distinctive silhouette of the original building.

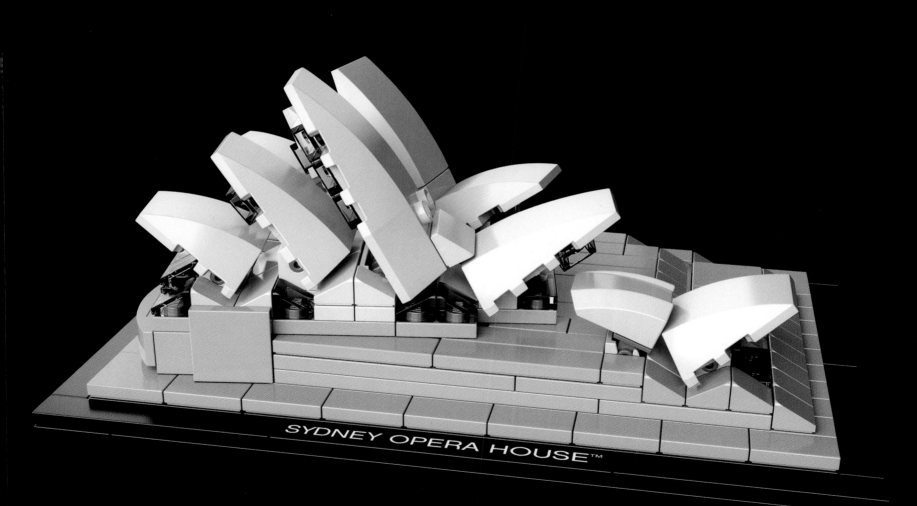

SYDNEY OPERA HOUSE™

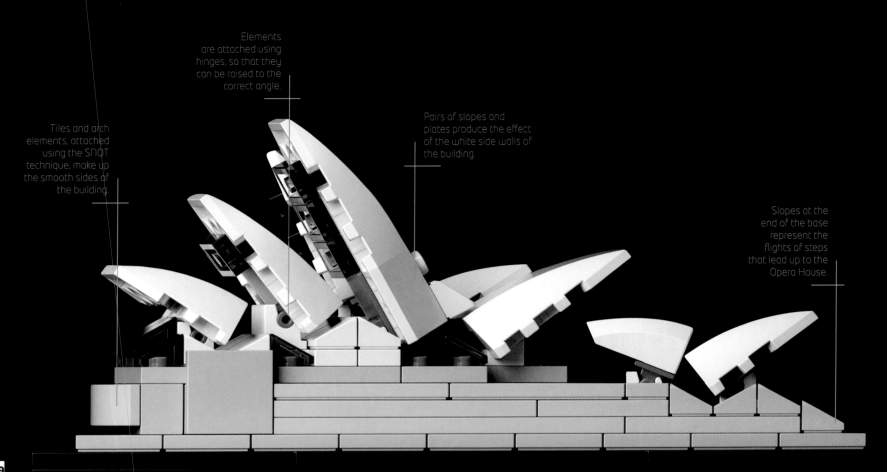

Elements
are attached using
hinges, so that they
can be raised to the
correct angle.

Pairs of slopes and
plates produce the effect
of the white side walls of
the building.

Tiles and arch
elements, attached
using the SNOT
technique, make up
the smooth sides of
the building.

Slopes at the
end of the base
represent the
flights of steps
that lead up to the
Opera House.

# THE MODEL

It was not only the famous sails that proved
difficult to recreate in LEGO bricks. Another
problem for the artist was that some of the
buildings are set at a slight angle to the
surrounding plaza. Construction at an angle
is further complicated because the terraces
around the buildings are at more than one level.
To enable the opera house and concert hall to
be positioned at the correct angle, Adam Reed
Tucker supported them on turntables set in the
base. These bricks are invisible in the finished
model and, as the surrounding terraces are
built of tiles, with no studs, the buildings seem
to float effortlessly, without any obvious
means of anchorage.

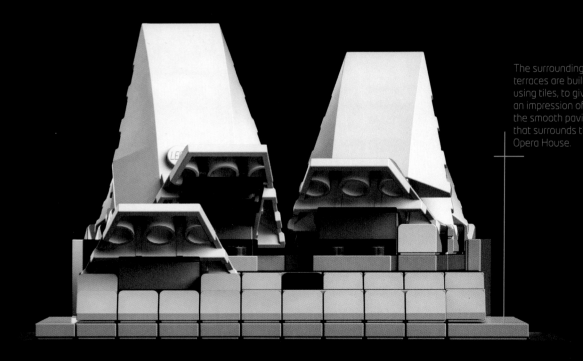

The surrounding
terraces are built
using tiles, to give
an impression of
the smooth paving
that surrounds the
Opera House.

### Model 21012

Most of the model's bricks are in two colours – white for the sails and some side walls, beige for the lower parts of the building and surrounding podium. This colour relationship is strikingly true to the original building.

**LEGO artist** Adam Reed Tucker
**LEGO builder** Steen Sig Andersen
**LEGO bricks** 270
**Building steps** 57
**Dimensions** 160 x 70 mm
**Release date** 2012

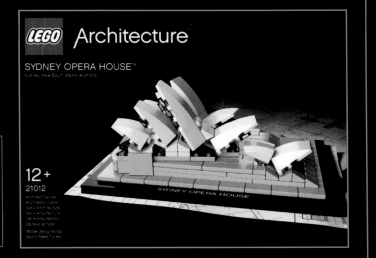

**LEGO** Architecture

SYDNEY OPERA HOUSE™
Sydney, New South Wales, Australia

12+
21012

The white elements that make up the sails are more commonly seen with all their connection points used when representing the fuselages of aircraft or the legs of the character Buzz Lightyear.

Transparent slopes and plates produce the effect of the large glazed areas beneath the roof sails.

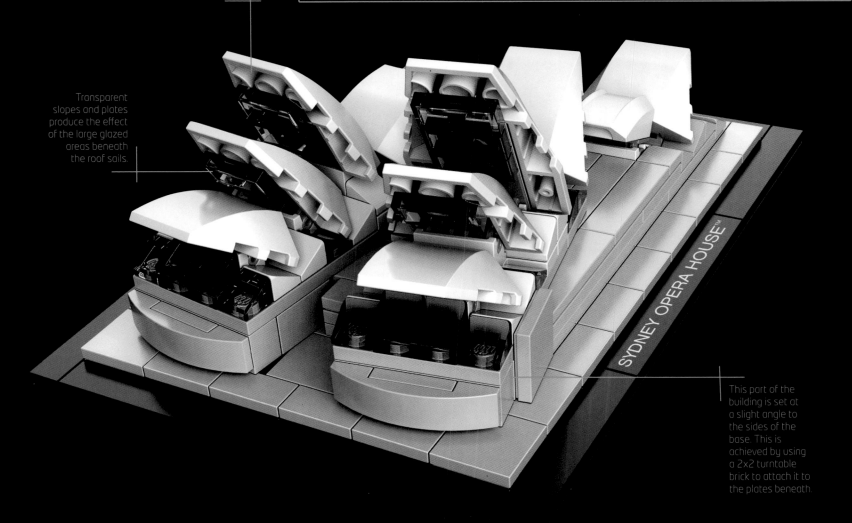

This part of the building is set at a slight angle to the sides of the base. This is achieved by using a 2x2 turntable brick to attach it to the plates beneath.

**Jørn Utzon**
**(1918–2008)**
Prior to winning the competition to design the Sydney Opera House™, Utzon had primarily designed small houses in his native Denmark. His later work includes a wide range of buildings, from housing schemes and a church, to the National Assembly Building in Kuwait. Utzon's work combines modern materials with inspiration from, and respect for, nature – he said that a design should grow naturally, like a tree.

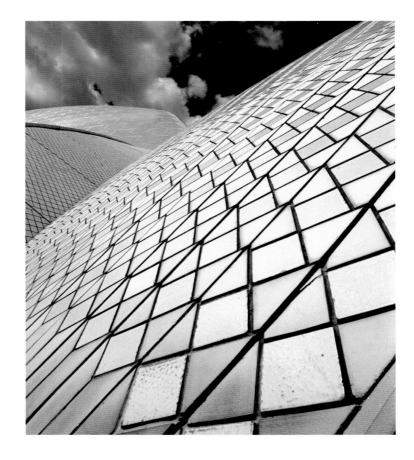

**Stunning Tiles**
Specially designed glossy white and matt cream ceramic tiles on the sails make the building stand out against the surrounding podium and water.

# THE ORIGINAL

**A Waterfront Masterpiece**
The Opera House is set on a promontory in Sydney Harbour called Bennelong Point. Its namesake, Bennelong, was an important intermediary between the local Aborigines and settlers. It now provides a perfect site for the Opera House, which is almost surrounded by water.

In 1956 the government of New South Wales announced a competition for the design of a new opera house and concert venue in Sydney. A year later, Jørn Utzon's design was declared the winner, from 233 entries. The design, with its sculptural, shell-shaped sails, was outstanding, but required further work on the construction details. Construction began in 1959, while architect and engineers continued to determine exactly how to build the unusual structure. By the late 1960s, the extraordinary silhouette had taken form and in 1973 the Opera House was opened. Since then the building has been widely admired, most notably for its sails, the largest of which is as tall as a 20-storey building. Other successful elements include the vast expanses of glass that enable opera-goers to look out over Sydney Harbour from the theatre foyers. Visitors enjoy the well-appointed interiors, although these were not built without challenges – acoustics, backstage facilities and other requirements were all considered during the construction process. The effort was worthwhile however, and the building is popular with performers and visitors alike.

# BIG BEN

**A Landmark in Stone**

The tower was originally built of limestone from Yorkshire, a sandy-coloured stone that was quite soft and wore away rapidly as a result of atmospheric pollution. Much of this material was replaced in the 20th century with more durable limestone from a different British quarry, producing the warm, honey-coloured surface that remains today. Rok Zgalin Kobe chose to recreate this surface with beige LEGO® bricks, using grey for the roofs.

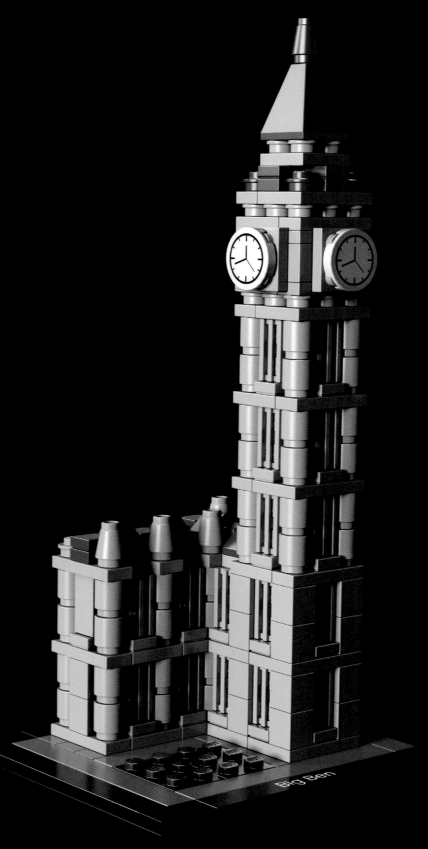

Big Ben

# BIG BEN

## LEGO® Artist: Rok Zgalin Kobe

Home to Britain's Houses of Parliament, London's Palace of Westminster was built in the Gothic style during the 1840s and 1850s. Its most famous part is the clock tower, which is often known as Big Ben although this is actually the name of the large bell inside that strikes the hours. The tower's official name, since the Diamond Jubilee of Queen Elizabeth II in 2012, is the Elizabeth Tower. The clock tower is one of London's most famous buildings, a notable landmark next to Parliament Square and Westminster Bridge and a symbol both of the city and of Britain as a whole. Rok Zgalin Kobe was above all keen to recreate the tower's shape, so that the model would be instantly recognisable as a recreation of this familiar structure. The tower's distinctive form comes from the way the architects divided it into three main parts – the bottom two storeys, the tall central section, and the upper part consisting of the clock faces and roof. By treating each of the sections slightly differently, the model gives a clear impression of the tower's three-part construction, which resembles a column with its base and capital, without being a literal copy of the building. Including a small part of the adjoining Parliament building also enabled the artist to show how the tower is linked to this larger structure.

The clock tower forms a notable landmark at one end of London's Westminster Bridge.

**Building** "Big Ben" (Elizabeth Tower), Palace of Westminster
**Architects** Sir Charles Barry and A. W. N. Pugin
**Location** London, England
**Building type** Government building and clock tower

**Year** 1843–1860
**Construction type** Brickwork faced with stone and iron-framed spire
**Height** 96 m
**Square footage** 17,000 sq. ft
**Architecture style** Gothic revival

*"The model recreates the overall architectural layout of the tower, while also paying attention to the texture of its walls and windows".*

**Rok Zgalin Kobe**

# THE MODEL

The clock tower is a large, elaborate structure, and is full of intricate detail that is too small to reproduce in a small-scale LEGO model. The artist therefore decided to recreate the overall texture of the exterior, which is one of the most important aspects of the building's design. This texture is made up of a graphic contrast between vertical elements (including the upward-pointing, spire-like roof and slender profile), and a number of strong horizontal features. In the real building, the most obvious horizontals are bands of stone running right across the building, dividing it up into horizontal sections. The LEGO model recreates these with layers of plates. The way they contrast with the vertical elements (such as the grilles that make up the windows) produces an effective representation of the original building's intricate surface texture. Further vertical features, including the pinnacles and the upper part of the roof, harmonise with this arrangement.

Small double-slope bricks create the sense of a pitched roof behind the pinnacles of the Houses of Parliament.

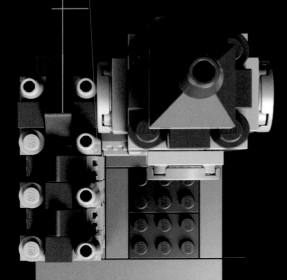

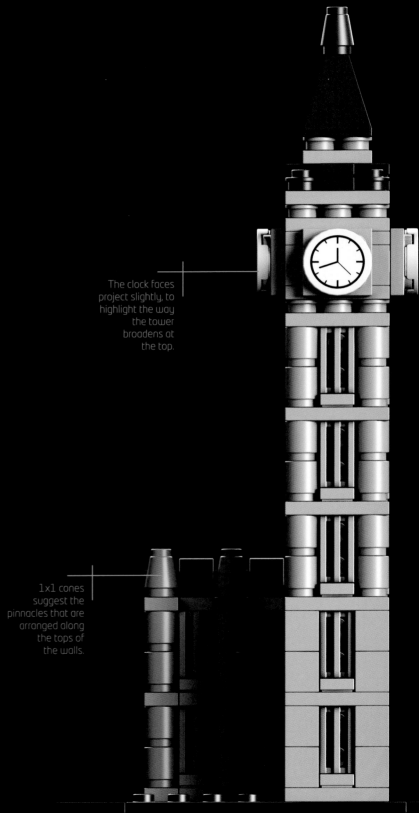

The clock faces project slightly, to highlight the way the tower broadens at the top.

1x1 cones suggest the pinnacles that are arranged along the tops of the walls.

Without reproducing the shape of the roof exactly, this grey slope, topped with a 1x1 cone, gives the impression of the way it comes to a point.

A patch of green tiles symbolises the garden that runs along the side of the Houses of Parliament.

**Model 21013**
The completed model reproduces the overall structure of the tower, with its three-part base-column-capital layout. It manages to do this without reproducing the proportions precisely, which would have been impossible using LEGO bricks at this scale.

**LEGO artist** Rok Zgalin Kobe
**LEGO builder** Steen Sig Andersen
**LEGO bricks** 346
**Building steps** 52
**Dimensions** 96 x 196 mm
**Release date** 2012

*LEGO* Architecture

**Big Ben**
London, Great Britain

12+
21013

Landmark Series
Sehenswürdigkeiten
Série Monuments
Serie Monumental
Serie Edificios
Históricos
Nevezetes helyek
sorozat

Model designed by
Rok Zgalin Kobe

Layers of plates give a sense of the horizontal divisions that are a key feature of the tower's architecture.

# IN FOCUS

An ingenious way of portraying the complex surface of the tower was to use components that create patterns of light and shade. In the upper section, the artist achieved this using layers made up of 1x1 round bricks above and below the clock face and in the pointed roof. The effect of light and shade was also enhanced through the use of grilles to represent windows. The result is a representation of the kinds of patterns that are often found in English architecture of the late Middle Ages, and which the architects, Barry and Pugin, were reviving in their design for the Houses of Parliament.

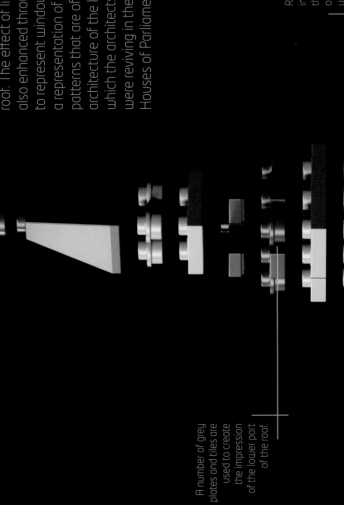
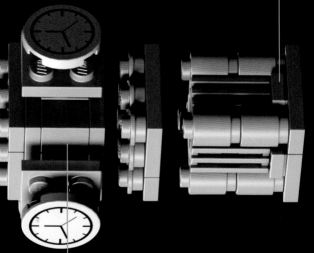

Round plates recreate in simplified form the intricate design of the tower's upper section.

A small tile beneath the grille suggests a window sill.

A number of grey plates and tiles are used to create the impression of the lower part of the roof.

The clock faces fit on to 2x2 tiles using the SNOT building technique.

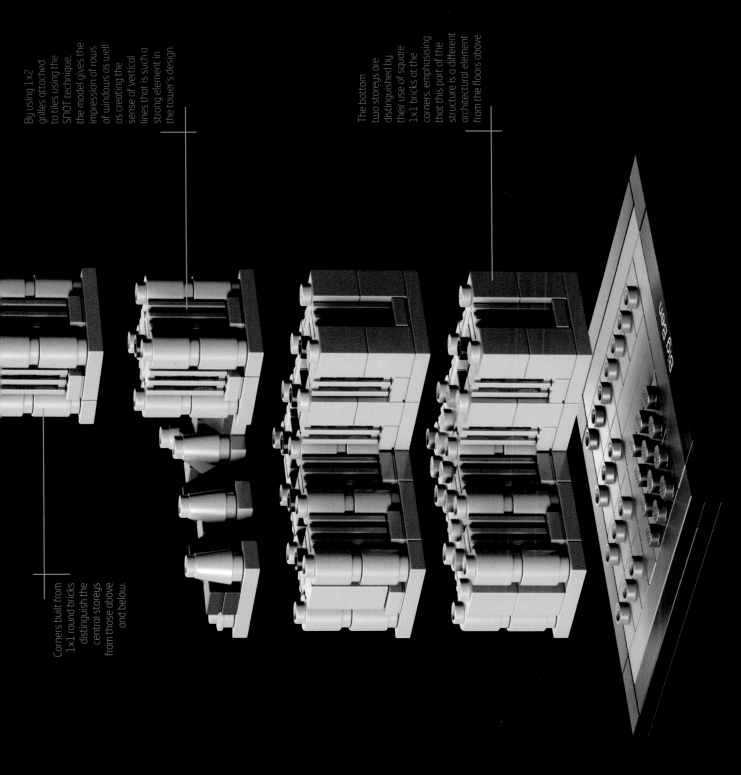

By using 1x2
grilles attached
to tiles using the
SNOT technique,
the model gives the
impression of rows
of windows as well
as creating the
sense of vertical
lines that is such a
strong element in
the tower's design.

The bottom
two storeys are
distinguished by
their use of square
1x1 bricks at the
corners, emphasising
that this part of the
structure is a different
architectural element
from the floors above.

Corners built from
1x1 round bricks
distinguish the
central storeys
from those above
and below.

**The Great Clock Face**
The clock has four faces, each 7 metres in diameter, with black cast-iron hour figures half a metre in height. The dials are glazed with opal glass and illuminated from within, so that passers-by can read the time during the hours of darkness.

# THE ORIGINAL

In 1834, the Palace of Westminster, home of Britain's Houses of Parliament, was destroyed in a fire. The government invited architects to submit plans for a replacement and settled on a design by Sir Charles Barry, who planned a vast building in the Gothic style on the bank of the River Thames. Barry enlisted the help of fellow architect, A. W. N. Pugin, who was an expert in the Gothic style and provided designs for many of the details and decorations in the building, from carvings to wallpapers. Pugin was also responsible for designing the clock tower, conceiving its distinctive profile and the meticulous decorative detail around the clock face. Although compatible with the Gothic Revival style of the rest of the building, the tower is a unique design. A strong punctuation mark at one end of the building, the vertical lines running up its walls and the distinctive pointed roof make it look even taller than it is. The clock was started in 1859 and the chimes and the bell known as Big Ben quickly became familiar. By the 20th century, the tower had become a national symbol, the clock set the time for the nation, and Pugin's Gothic masterpiece was known all over the world.

**A River View**
The south front of the Houses of Parliament looks out over the River Thames. The clock tower rises above this part of the building, creating an imposing landmark even from quite distant viewpoints across the river.

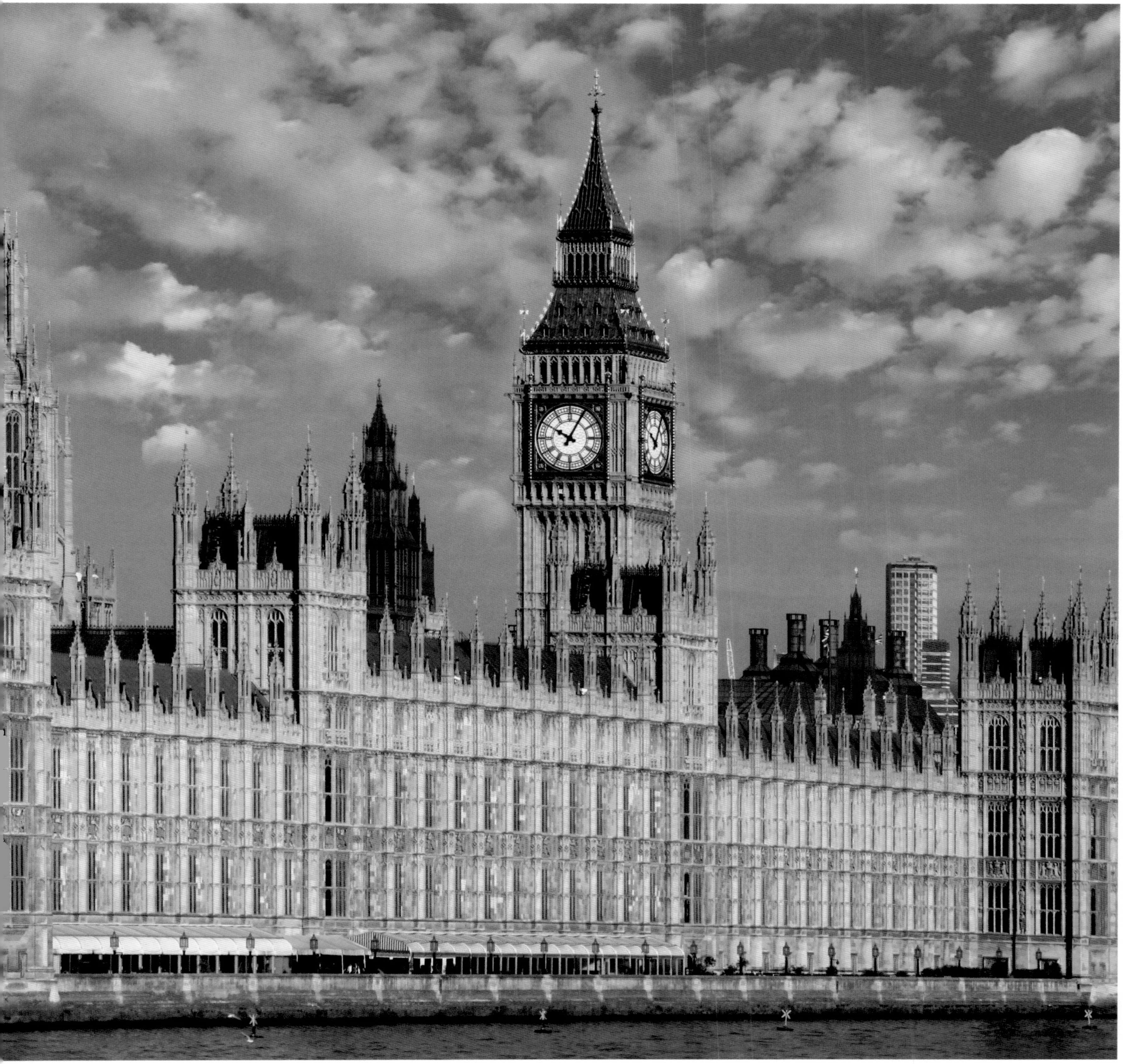

# VILLA SAVOYE

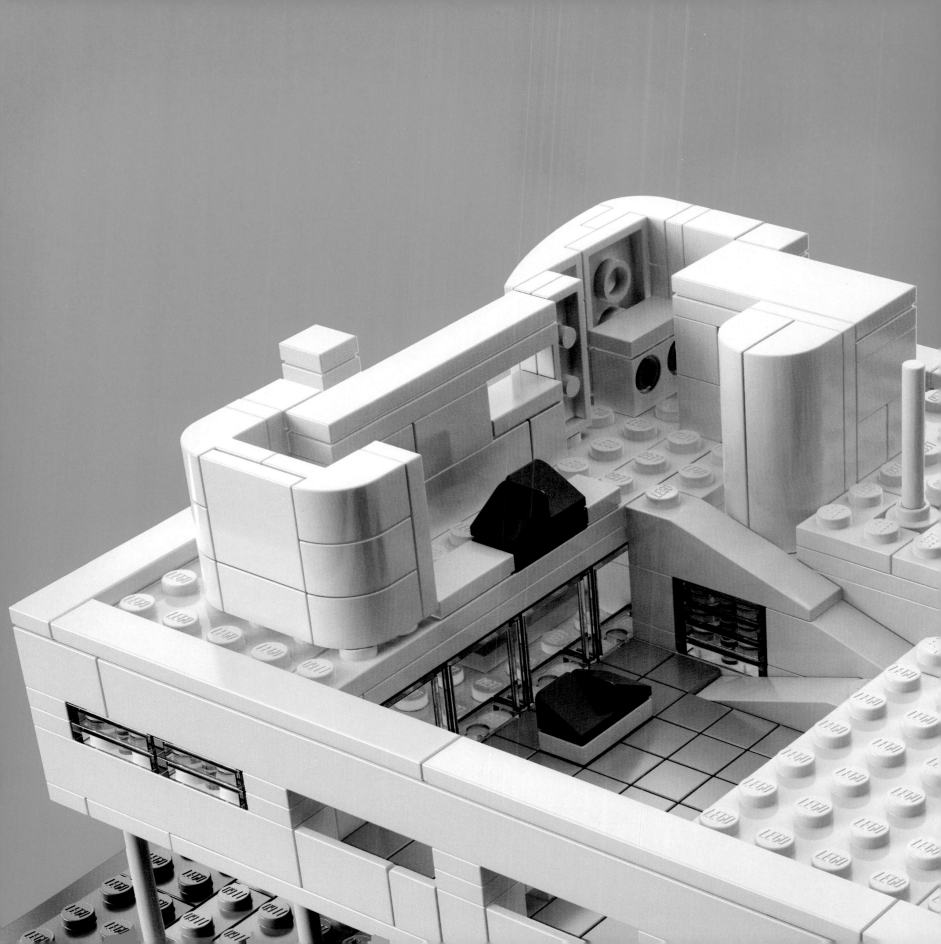

## A Study in White

The overall impression created by the Villa Savoye, especially since its recent restoration, is one of carefully finished surfaces of smooth, white concrete. By using long bricks and tiles, with as few joins as possible between them, the LEGO® artist and builder were able to represent these immaculate surfaces.

# VILLA SAVOYE

**LEGO® Artist: Michael Hepp**

Set among lawns on the outskirts of Paris, the Villa Savoye is one of the masterpieces of the Swiss architect Le Corbusier and a key building in the history of modern architecture. Although the plain white walls of the house seem ideal for recreation in LEGO bricks, the building was not as easy to model as it looks. This is in part because the building is full of contrasts and apparent contradictions – for example, although the house seems very simple in form from the side, when looked at from above there are many telling and important details, such as the terrace, its long ramp and the complex structures that form the top floor, none of which was straightforward to recreate. The challenges were greater still because Le Corbusier worked out the original building's proportions so carefully – even a slight change led to a model that seemed unbalanced, so the team tried to get as close as they could to the architect's original proportions. The resulting model was the fruit of a close collaboration between LEGO artist Michael Hepp and LEGO builder Steen Sig Andersen, with the builder coming up with the idea of using rods to represent the all-important pilotis (columns) on which the building stands. This solution is more true to scale than making these using 1x1 bricks, as the artist originally proposed. It ensures that the overall proportions of the model come close to those of Le Corbusier's masterpiece.

Villa Savoye is widely thought of as the seminal work of Le Corbusier.

**Building** Villa Savoye
**Architect** Le Corbusier and Pierre Jeanneret
**Location** Poissy, Paris, France
**Building type** House

**Year** 1928–1931
**Construction type** Reinforced concrete with post and beam structure
**Height** 9.4 m
**Square footage** 4,392 sq. ft
**Architecture style** Modernist

*"Le Corbusier has always been an inspiration to me. His architecture is harmonious, well balanced and coherent".*

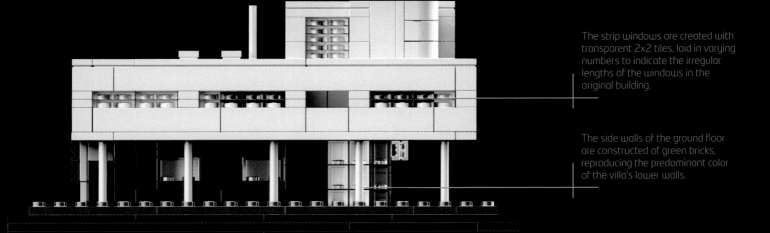

The strip windows are created with transparent 2x2 tiles, laid in varying numbers to indicate the irregular lengths of the windows in the original building.

The side walls of the ground floor are constructed of green bricks, reproducing the predominant color of the villa's lower walls.

# THE MODEL

The main challenges in designing the model were to choose the right scale and to find LEGO bricks that could represent some of the more unusual, sculptural parts of the building. The structures on the roof, with their complex curves, the gently sloping ramp and the strip windows all posed challenges, especially as the balance and poise of the original building meant that changes in the model's proportions could spoil its effect. However, careful selection of bricks eventually led to a result that was true to the spirit of the original.

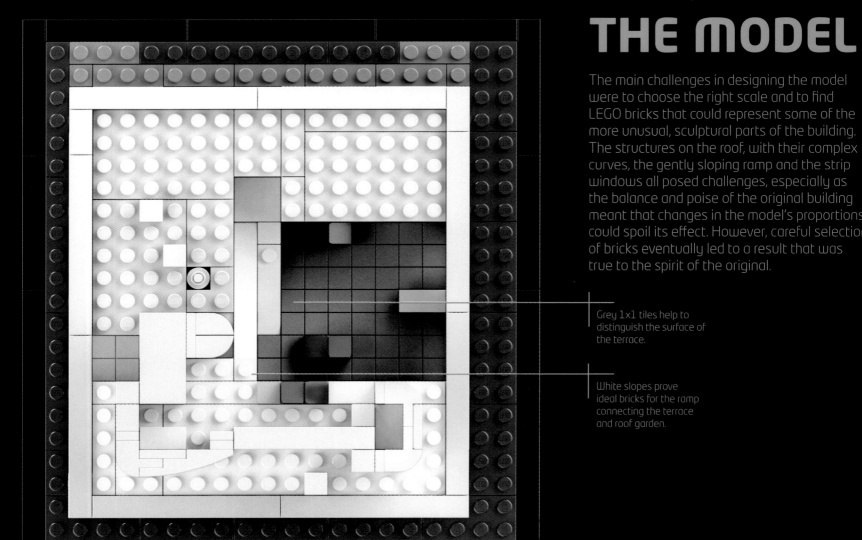

Grey 1x1 tiles help to distinguish the surface of the terrace.

White slopes prove ideal bricks for the ramp connecting the terrace and roof garden.

A handful of green bricks represent the planting in the terrace and roof garden.

**Model 21014**
The mainly white model rises on its slender pilotis above a base edged with green tiles, which symbolize the lawns that surround the original house.

**LEGO** Architecture

Villa Savoye
Poissy, France

**LEGO artist** Michael Hepp
**LEGO builder** Steen Sig Andersen
**LEGO bricks** 660
**Building steps** 75
**Dimensions** 192 x 92 mm
**Release date** 2012

12+
21014

An ingenious combination of curved half-arches, curved bricks and other bricks makes up the complex structure on the roof of the building.

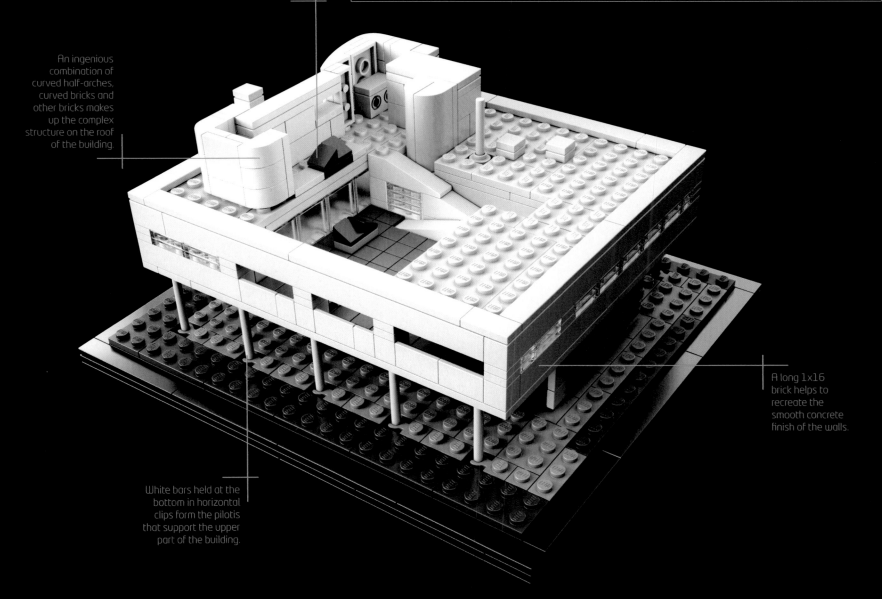

A long 1x16 brick helps to recreate the smooth concrete finish of the walls.

White bars held at the bottom in horizontal clips form the pilotis that support the upper part of the building.

**Inside Out**
The interior and terrace are separated only by a floor-to-ceiling screen of glass, so that the two spaces merge together. The continuous line of the strip windows enhances this effect.

# THE ORIGINAL

The Villa Savoye is one of several houses that the architect and his cousin Pierre Jeanneret designed in the 1920s, in which Le Corbusier perfected his idea of a pure, white-walled architecture. He listed five key points or features that such a building should have: it should be raised above the ground on columns or "pilotis"; it should have a free floor plan, with non-structural walls dividing the interior spaces; the facades should also be free and asymmetrical; there should be long horizontal strip windows and the house should have a roof garden. The Villa brings the five points together to create a structure of extraordinary grace and sophistication. The building seems to hover over the ground, and the strip windows, terrace and seamless interior spaces produce one of the most light and airy houses ever built.

**A Seamless Facade**
The building's exterior is a harmonious blend of curves and straight lines, solids and voids. The main floor's strip windows make the building partly transparent. By contrast, the upper floor is all sinuous curves with concrete walls giving privacy to the occupants.

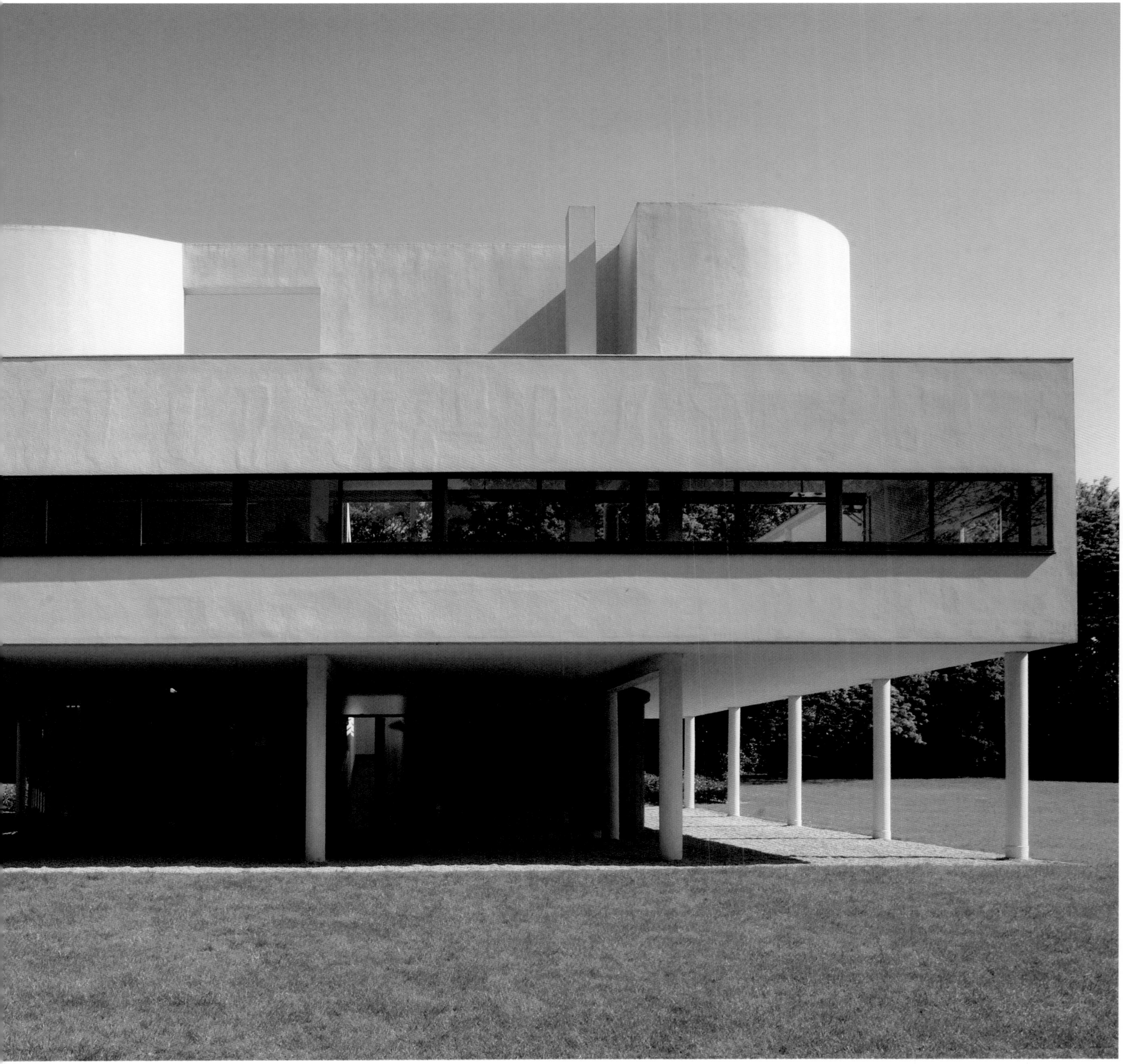

# SUNGNYEMUN

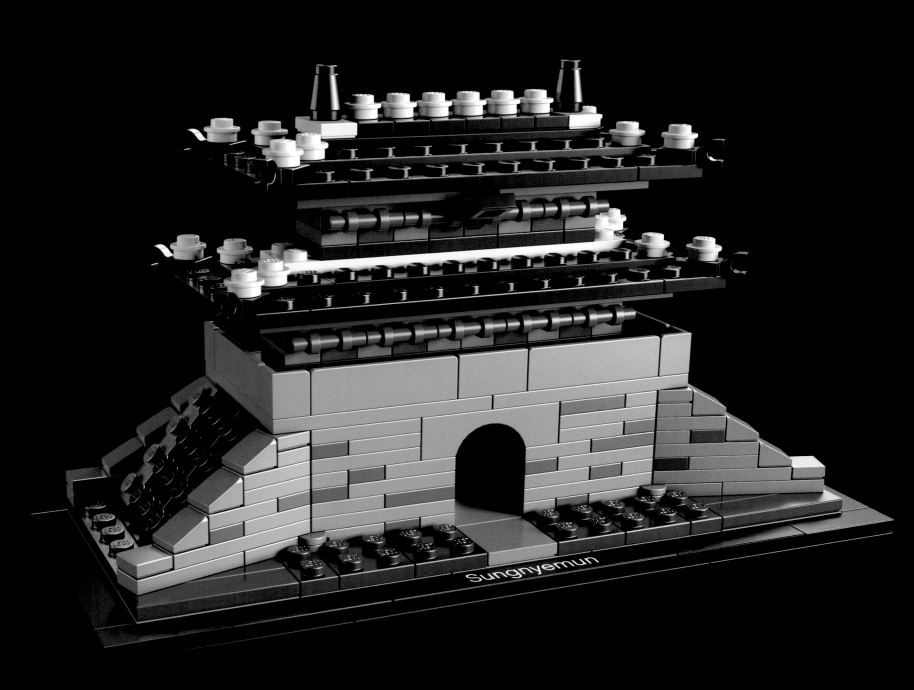

Sungnyemun

# SUNGNYEMUN

## LEGO® Artist: Adam Reed Tucker

Officially designated as South Korea's first National Treasure, Sungnyemun is a magnificent 14th-century city gate in Seoul. Originally part of Seoul's ancient defensive walls, it is now in the middle of the city and surrounded by modern buildings. It consists of a massive stone lower section, designed to protect Seoul's inhabitants from enemies and prowling tigers, topped with an elaborate double roof that has an upturned, pagoda-style shape and was designed to mark the structure as one of the most important entrances into the city. Virtually every aspect of Sungnyemun, from the angles and curves of its walls and roofs to the intricate woodwork of its upper storeys, was difficult to recreate using LEGO bricks. By carefully varying the color of the LEGO bricks used in the model, Adam Reed Tucker managed to bring out the character of the building's materials, recreating the striking contrast between the rugged stone base and the more delicate carpentry of the upper parts, while also achieving a shape that reflects the complex lines of the original without trying to copy them literally.

A grand entrance to Seoul.

**Building** Sungnyemun
**Architect** Unknown
**Location** Seoul, South Korea
**Building type** City gate
**Year** 1396–1398; rebuilt 1447, 1479; major restoration 2013

**Construction type** Stone masonry base with wooden upper storeys
**Height** 15.8 m
**Square footage** 51,000 sq. ft
**Architecture style** Joseon

*"The model aims to capture the essential features of Asian architecture, especially in terms of colour, texture and form".*

Adam Reed Tucker

# THE MODEL

To model the roof of Sungnyemun, the artist had two main challenges: to find a way of suggesting the roof's gently curving lines and to work out how to represent the nobbly surfaces of the tiles and finials. The upturned curve of the roof is conveyed very subtly, by adding a 1x1 plate with a clip at each corner, angled so that the clip is set at a diagonal to the sides of the building. The roof's rough surface is portrayed using plates, so that the studs are visible, with the addition of white round plates to give extra texture and suggest finials.

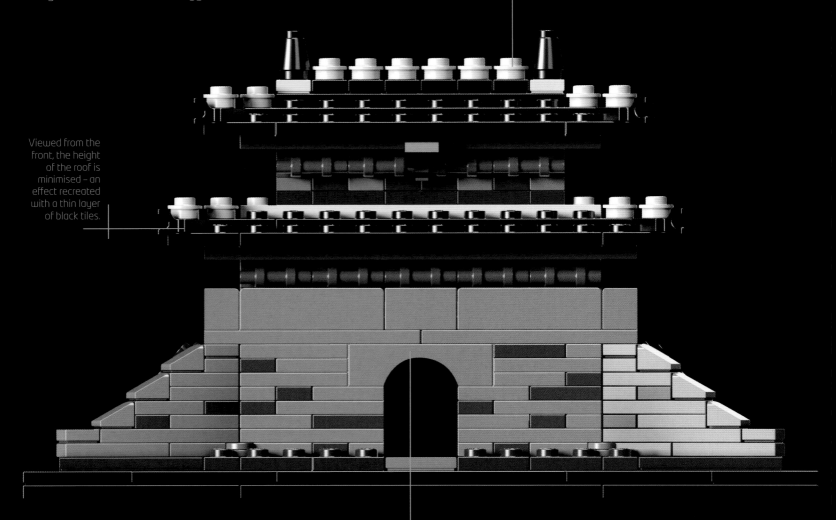

White 1x1 round plates help to suggest the studded surface of the gateway's roof.

Viewed from the front, the height of the roof is minimised – an effect recreated with a thin layer of black tiles.

At this scale, a 1x4 round arch makes the ideal LEGO brick for the entrance to the gateway.

## Model 21016

Although the model does not reproduce the shape of the original building exactly, it is still unmistakeably an oriental structure with overhanging, pagoda-like roofs.

**LEGO artist** Adam Reed Tucker
**LEGO builder** Steen Sig Andersen
**LEGO bricks** 325
**Building steps** 53
**Dimensions** 175 x 105 mm
**Release date** 2012

The main body of the upper section is built up using plates just two studs deep.

The roof elements are deeper than the masonry beneath, stepping outwards to produce the effect of the roof's generous overhang.

Angled plates produce a sense of depth at the top of the stone walls.

# IN FOCUS

One of the striking things about Sungnyemun's structure is the contrast between the narrow superstructure with the broad base and the overhanging roofs. LEGO bricks, with their vast range of sizes, were ideal to recreate this aspect of the design. Even at the model's small scale, Adam Reed Tucker was able to vary the depth from six studs for the base to just two studs for parts of the upper section to give a clear sense of the structure's varying profile.

A 1x1 cone represents one of the prominent finials that break up the gateway's roof line.

A plate with a clip, set at an angle, suggests the upturned corner of the roof.

Grey plates form the roof's underside.

A combination of colored plates arranged to form a pattern symbolises the elaborately painted woodwork of the structure immediately beneath the roof.

A grey bar, held in a series of clips, represents the carved carpentry of the structure.

Colour variation in the tiles that make up the wall suggest the rugged quality of the masonry.

A series of grey tiles depicts the roadway through the arch.

A grey hinge enables the buttress to be set at angle to the rest of the structure.

This green plate, supported at an angle with the help of a hinge, produces the effect of a grassy bank.

**A National Treasure Restored**
The gate was badly damaged in the 1950s during the Korean War, after which it was restored. A fire in 2008 destroyed all the wooden parts, but the gate has now been reconstructed using traditional tools and techniques, ensuring that the building is once again one of the foremost examples of the architecture of Korea's Joseon period.

# THE ORIGINAL

In 1392, King Taejo came to power in Korea, marking the beginning of some 500 years of rule by the Joseon dynasty. Taejo relocated the capital to Hanseong (modern Seoul) and fortified the city with strong stone walls pierced by a series of eight gates. The largest and most elaborate of these gates was originally called Namdaemun (Great Southern Gate), although it is now generally known as Sungnyemun (Gate of Exalted Ceremonies), recalling the time when it was the place where foreign dignitaries were formally greeted when they arrived in the city.

The structure of the gate was modified during the 15th century, and it was then that it took its current form, with its stone lower walls topped by an elaborate wooden structure of beams and struts supporting twin upturned roofs. Joseon palaces, fortresses, temples and other notable buildings had similar eye-catching overhanging roofs, which marked them out as structures of importance and prestige. The roof of Sungnyemun was the oldest timber building in Korea until its wooden parts were destroyed by fire in 2008.

**In the Modern City**
In 1907 the stone walls on either side of Sungnyemun were demolished to improve traffic flow and to allow a tramway to pass the gate. Sungnyemun is now isolated on an island of grass, with roads passing on either side and the gate, which was once the tallest building in Seoul, is now dwarfed by the tall modern buildings around it.

# THE LEANING TOWER OF PISA

## A Three-Part Tower With A Tilt

The tower consists of three main sections. At the base is the tall, thick-walled ground storey, represented in the model by 1x1 bricks topped with arches. Next come the six storeys that make up most of the tower, all of which are surrounded by rows of round-topped arches, each level consisting of arches supported by pairs of round bricks. At the top is the third section, the belfry, which is narrower than the rest of the tower and is made up mainly of round bricks. The model gets quite close to the proportions of the real tower without copying its structure slavishly.

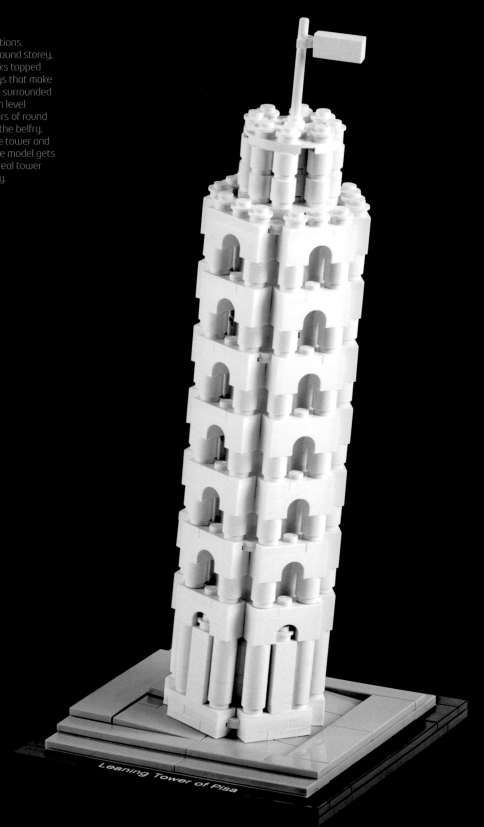

Leaning Tower of Pisa

# THE LEANING TOWER OF PISA

**LEGO® Artist: Adam Reed Tucker**

The bell tower of the cathedral of Pisa was begun in 1173. Its stunning structure in white marble, lined with arches for much of its height, makes it instantly recognisable. Even before the tower was completed, it acquired its most famous feature. The structure began to lean because the foundation was not strong enough to support it on one side where the ground was soft. Reproducing the lean proved difficult for Adam Reed Tucker, the artist who created this model, because all LEGO® bricks are designed to be assembled vertically. An ingenious construction technique was therefore required for the base of the model, so that the tower could lean while also remaining stable.

The other challenge was to recreate the circular building using mainly straight-sided bricks, while also keeping the model at a manageable scale. To maintain a fairly compact size, the artist decided to use a small arch brick as the principal element of the six main storeys of building's exterior. At the resulting scale, he found that the best way to produce an impression of a round building was to give the model a five-sided plan. Although the model is not literally round, it still proves to be easily recognisable as the celebrated leaning tower.

From close to the tower, the ornate masonry of the bottom storey is clearly visible.

**Building** The Leaning Tower of Pisa
**Architect** Unknown; possibly Master Diotisalvi, with Nicola and Giovanni Pisano
**Location** Pisa, Italy
**Building type** Bell tower

**Year** 1173-1372
**Construction type** Solid limestone walls faced with marble
**Height** 55.86 m
**Square footage** Approx. 11,000 sq. ft
**Architecture style** Romanesque

*"To make sides three studs long using 1x2 hinged plates, I had to stagger the hinged plates, fitting them at different levels to produce sides of the right length".*

**Adam Reed Tucker**

## Model 21015

The marble-clad walls of the tower made it easy to decide on the color of the model. White LEGO bricks and plates were the obvious choice.

**LEGO artist** Adam Reed Tucker
**LEGO builder** Steen Sig Andersen
**LEGO bricks** 345
**Building steps** 65
**Dimensions** 112 x 259 mm
**Release date** 2013

# THE MODEL

To make the tower lean the correct amount, one side needed to be raised by the depth of a single plate. The artist attached the bottom of this higher side of the tower to a plate fixed to the model's base using a hinged brick, so that the structure can sit at an angle. The other side of the tower is not physically attached to the base, but rests on a tile. The effect is as if the lower side of the tower has sunk slightly in the ground, which is exactly what happened to the real building during its construction.

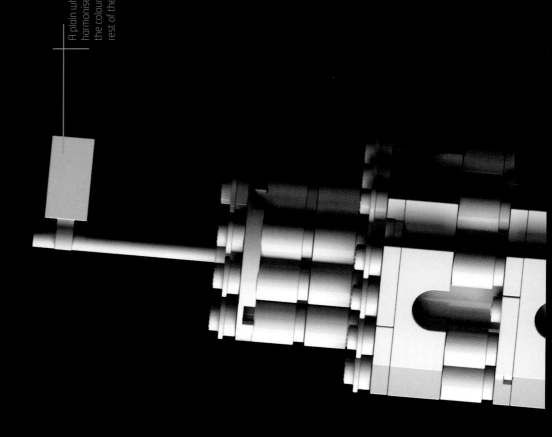

A plain white flag harmonises with the colour of the rest of the model.

Leaning Tower of Pisa

Hinged plates make possible the angles necessary to make the five-sided structure.

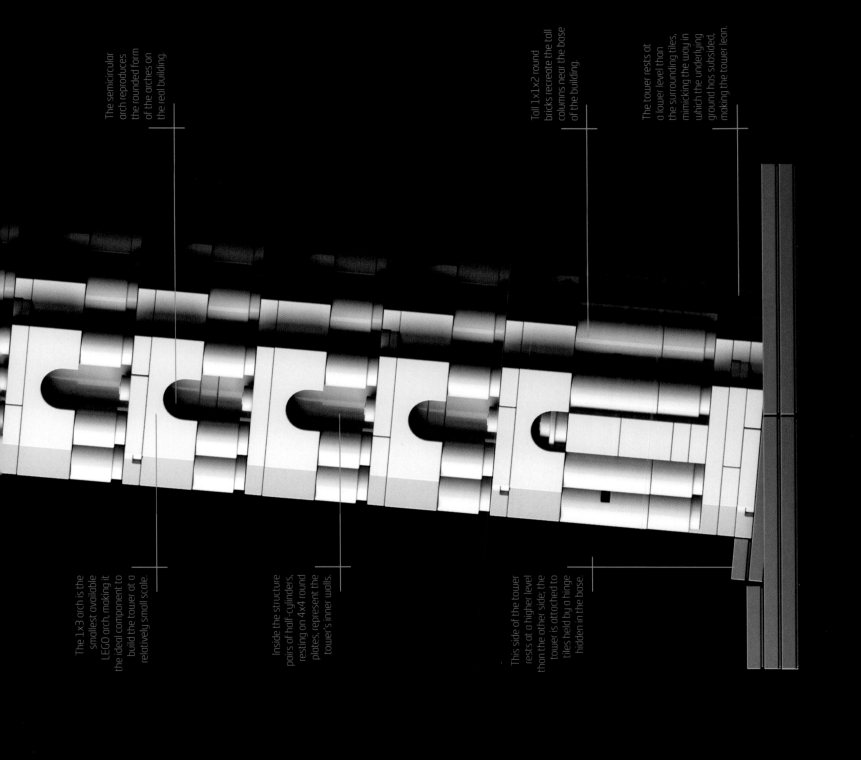

The semicircular arch reproduces the rounded form of the arches on the real building.

Tall 1x1x2 round bricks recreate the tall columns near the base of the building.

The tower rests at a lower level than the surrounding tiles, mimicking the way in which the underlying ground has subsided, making the tower lean.

The 1x3 arch is the smallest available LEGO arch, making it the ideal component to build the tower at a relatively small scale.

Inside the structure pairs of half-cylinders, resting on 4x4 round plates, represent the tower's inner walls.

This side of the tower rests at a higher level than the other side; the tower is attached to tiles held by a hinge hidden in the base.

### The Architect

No one knows for sure who designed the tower. It may well have been the work of Diotisalvi, a Pisa-born architect who designed the baptistery, another circular building adjacent to the city's cathedral. It is thought that Nicola Pisano and his son Giovanni, architects and sculptors who worked in Pisa and other Italian cites, may have supervised the later work.

**Romanesque Details**

The exterior of the tower is beautifully detailed. Its Romanesque semicircular arches are supported by marble columns topped with carved capitals. Between each row of arches is an elaborately carved cornice that marks each of the eight storeys.

# THE ORIGINAL

The Tower of Pisa was begun in 1173, as a detached bell tower for the nearby cathedral. A few years later, when the builders reached the second floor, they stopped work because the structure was sinking on one side. The main part of the tower was completed between 1272 and 1319; the belfry at the top was added later, in 1372. The long construction process was interrupted by various wars between Pisa and its neighbouring city states, but the delays had a hidden benefit. If the masons had built the tower quickly, its unstable foundations would almost certainly have led to a collapse. The builders matched the style of the nearby cathedral, using a similar white marble to face the walls and for the columns, and stuck to the round-arched Romanesque style used by the original masons. The upper floors were constructed so that they are slightly taller on one side than the other, to minimise the lean. In spite of this, and recent work to strengthen and stabilise the tower, it still leans by just under 4 degrees: the top of the tower is about 3.9 metres out of true.

**The Leaning Tower**

The Leaning Tower was built as a free-standing structure, next to the cathedral's transept. The tower's distinctive appearance is due both to the rows of arches on the galleries around the main floors and also to the large open arches of the belfry, which were designed to allow the sound of the bells to carry across the city.

# IMPERIAL HOTEL

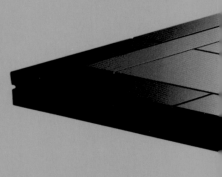

# IMPERIAL HOTEL

**LEGO® Artist: Rok Zgalin Kobe**

Tokyo's Imperial Hotel, designed by Frank Lloyd Wright, was a vast, sprawling building constructed between 1919 and 1923 and designed to withstand Japan's frequent earthquakes. Demolition of the hotel was completed in 1968, but the central section was disassembled and re-erected at Meiji-Mura, an architectural museum outside of Nagoya, Japan. The magnificent hotel lobby is the featured portion of the building that Rok Zgalin Kobe chose to recreate in the LEGO® model. Wright designed the hotel using a mix of materials including brick, concrete and carved stone, producing a striking three-colour contrast between the pink brick, grey concrete and dark carved Oya stone. The model does not reproduce these colors literally, but is faithful to the contrast effect, using beige bricks for the brickwork, and grey for the capstones and areas of carved stone. The low-pitched, green-patina copper roof of the original are interpreted using pale green LEGO slopes.

A major part of the building's visual impact comes from the lavish sculptural decoration on its walls and around the outside. Much of this decoration is in Oya stone – soft volcanic lava. The LEGO model interprets these carved surfaces in an abstract way, using small bricks such as 1x1 plates, to mimic the effect of the carving in such a small scale. These details, combined with the artist's close attention to the proportions of the building, make the model a faithful recreation of the original building.

The preserved central section of the original hotel is all that survives today.

**Building** Imperial Hotel
**Architect** Frank Lloyd Wright
**Location** Tokyo, Japan (surviving portion now relocated to Inuyama, near Nagoya, Japan)
**Building type** Hotel

**Year** 1919-1923
**Construction type** Solid walls of brick, concrete, and Oya stone on a floating foundation
**Architecture style** Designed by Wright, respectful of Japanese culture.

*"The model emphasises the Japanese character of the building, with its overhanging roofs and subtle planes".*

**Rok Zgalin Kobe**

## A Complex Structure

The Imperial Hotel is a highly complex building. In addition to the recessed centre block and two flanking wings, there are many smaller protrusions and projections, together with complicated roofs and parapets that overhang by different amounts in different places. The model manages to capture much of this detail, representing the way Wright managed to balance numerous horizontal planes (mostly made of grey tiles in the model) with the strong vertical lines of the hotel's numerous windows.

Imperial Hotel

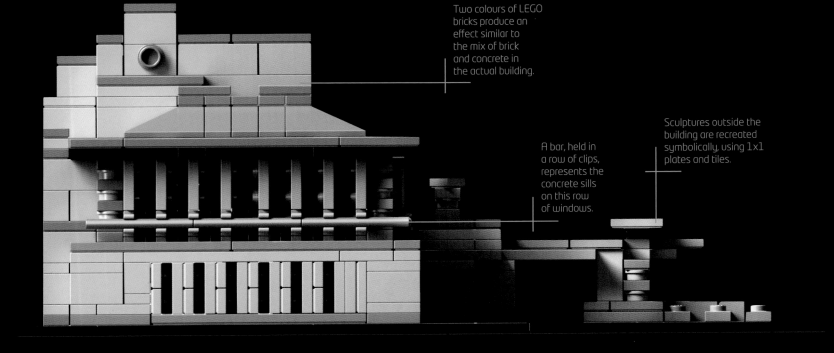

Two colours of LEGO bricks produce an effect similar to the mix of brick and concrete in the actual building.

A bar, held in a row of clips, represents the concrete sills on this row of windows.

Sculptures outside the building are recreated symbolically, using 1x1 plates and tiles.

# THE MODEL

One of the major decisions when creating the LEGO model was to choose the right scale. The sizes of elements such as the repeating windows produced standard modules that dictated the scale of the rest of the structure. These elements then had to be worked out in detail, often using fine adjustments such as small offsets to produce the right effect. Some of the transparent tiles that make up the windows have half-stud offsets so that the glazing is recessed. In other windows a similar effect is created by using bricks such as plates with slides.

The scale also affected the way the structure tapers. The actual building has heavy walls at the base and slightly lighter walls above. The model exaggerates this tapering slightly to make the effect clear. This kind of subtle exaggeration is also true of some of the aspects of the building that are influenced by Japanese architecture, notably the cantilevered roofs.

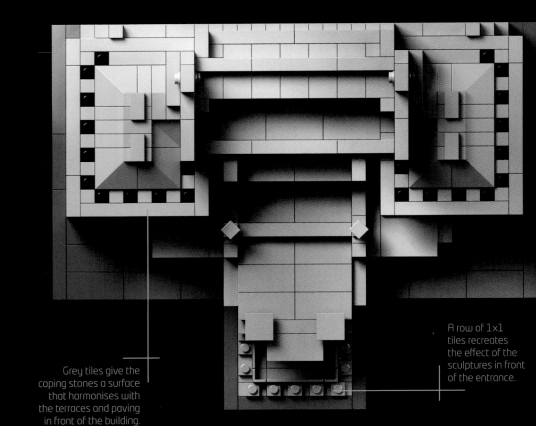

Grey tiles give the coping stones a surface that harmonises with the terraces and paving in front of the building.

A row of 1x1 tiles recreates the effect of the sculptures in front of the entrance.

## Model 21017

The model of the Imperial Hotel is one of the larger ones in the series, and uses its many small LEGO bricks to build a detailed impression of the building.

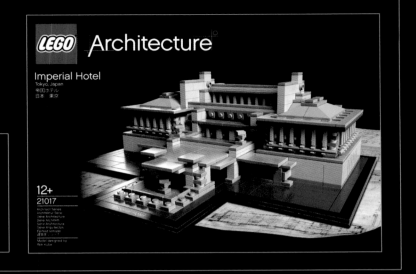

**LEGO** Architecture

**Imperial Hotel**
Tokyo, Japan
帝国ホテル
日本 東京

12+
21017

**LEGO artist** Rok Zgalin Kobe
**LEGO builder** Steen Sig Andersen
**LEGO bricks** 1,188
**Building steps** 104
**Dimensions** 288 x 105 mm
**Release date** 2013

Alternating round and square plates make up the corner piers, creating shadows that have a similar effect to the striped corner masonry of the actual building.

The protruding studs of these 1x1 plates represent the frieze above the hotel entrance.

The windows consist of transparent plates arranged on their sides between 1x2 plates with slides, using the SNOT technique.

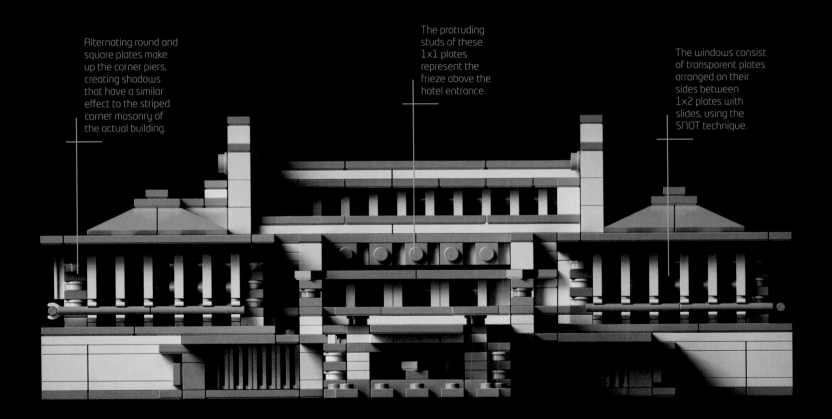

# THE ORIGINAL

In 1915, Tokyo's Imperial Hotel was no longer large enough to meet demand, and its owners commissioned American architect Frank Lloyd Wright to design a replacement. They wanted an architect who could bring a western approach to the building, but also someone who appreciated Japanese culture. Wright's design met these requirements, incorporating elements of Japanese architecture into his style.

Wright was aware of the potential for earthquakes in Japan and proposed shallow foundations so that the structure would "float" on the underlying alluvial mud and possibly withstand seismic activity. Separation joints throughout the building would prevent cracks from developing. On 1 September 1923, the day of the hotel's opening ceremony, a major earthquake struck. The building survived the quake, a triumph for Wright and a relief for the owners.

Wright's design was a masterpiece. From the outside it was a harmonious combination of cantilevered roofs, terraces, balconies and rows of windows. Inside, it featured well furnished public rooms adorned with striking stone carvings, and long corridors of guest rooms. The hotel remained popular until the mid-1960s, by which time it was too small and not modern enough to be financially viable.

**The Hotel Complex**
Wright's original building, seen in this photograph from 1935, was a complex structure. With its generous planting on the roof gardens, terraces, and around the pool, the effect was one of luxury and elegance. Following war damage and structural deterioration in the early 1960s, due to natural aging, it became necessary to demolish this iconic building. Today, the lobby section, which was disassembled and re-erected, is preserved, and can be visited at Museum Mieji-Mura.

# UNITED NATIONS HEADQUARTERS

**LEGO® Artist: Rok Zgalin Kobe**

The United Nations Headquarters in New York consists of a complex of several buildings set on an 18 acre site overlooking the East River. Two of the main structures – the General Assembly and Conference Buildings – have curved facades, so Rok Zgalin Kobe was faced not only with modeling a substantial group of large buildings at a small scale but also had to find a way of recreating their curves using mostly straight-sided bricks and plates. The buildings on the site are also very diverse – for example, the Secretariat Building, at 39 floors, is much taller than the others – so there was the additional issue of finding a scale that would work for all the structures. The most practical scale turned out to be one in which the height of one floor was roughly equivalent to that of a single plate or tile, a solution that enabled the artist to recreate the effect of the tower's glass curtain wall with a mixture of blue and transparent-blue plates. All the buildings in the model involve the use of the SNOT building technique, which not only helps in the creation of smooth wall surfaces but also allows more subtle variations in size than is possible when the bricks and plates are used the the conventional way.

The Secretariat tower is set back behind a plaza and the Dag Hammarskjöld Library.

**Building** United Nations Headquarters
**Architect** International team led by Wallace K. Harrison; main architect of final design, Oscar Niemeyer
**Location** New York City, U.S.A.
**Building type** Offices, assembly building, conference building, library

**Year** 1948–1952
**Construction type** Steel framework with glass curtain walls, plus additional elements in concrete.
**Height** 155 m (the Secretariat Building)
**Square footage** 784,080 sq. ft
**Architecture style** International modernist

*"Working out the relative sizes of the buildings and their details involved quite a lot of mathematics".*

**Rok Zgalin Kobe**

## A Variety of Elements

As well as making use of plates and tiles in a wider range of colours than is usual in the Architecture Series, the UN model also involves the ingenious recycling of a number of elements. These examples of creative recycling include the joysticks and the satellite dish used on the roof of the General Assembly Building.

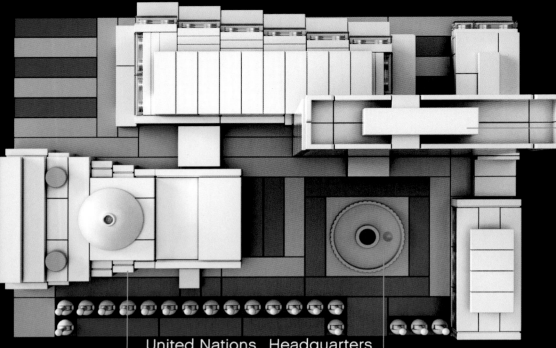

White angled tiles are used for the Tower's raised parapet.

United Nations   Headquarters

The SNOT technique allows the small offsets (the equivalent of the depth of half a LEGO plate) that symbolise the curvature in the walls of the General Assembly Building.

This turntable element represents the round fountain in front of the Secretariat tower.

White tiles set o top of transpare plates to create an overhang produce a faithf portrayal of the upper part of the Library's roo

Large white tiles set on their sides (held in place by hidden angled plates with studs facing downwards) recreate the smooth white facades of the tower.

# THE MODEL

The architecture of the UN Headquarters blends the simplicity of the International Style, with its walls of glass and expanses of concrete, with a more sculptural approach. The buildings are clean and deceptively simple in appearance, but recreating them involved some complex LEGO building techniques. For example, the main glazed part of the Secretariat Building's facade is eight studs across, but the tiles that clad the sides add an extra stud to the building's width. Making it possible to build the parapet on top of the tower, now nine studs wide, involved the use of a lot of small bricks, some concealed from view in the completed model, so that the finished effect looks effortless.

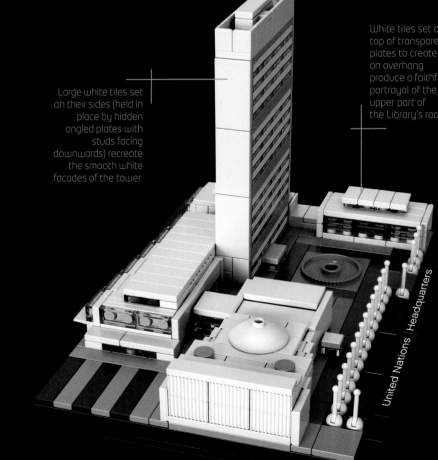

United Nations  Headquarters

**Model 21018**
The UN Headquarters model is very successful in bringing together a lot of small details – from flagpoles to glazing – to make a strong final effect.

**LEGO artist** Rok Zgalin Kobe
**LEGO builder** Steen Sig Andersen
**LEGO bricks** 597
**Building steps** 74
**Dimensions** 208 x 138 mm
**Release date** 2013

**LEGO** Architecture

United Nations Headquarters
New York City NY USA

Ages/edades
**12+**
21018
**597 pcs/ pzs**

Landmark Series
Serie edifices historiques
Serie Monumental

Model designed by
Rok Kobe

Building Toy
Jouet de Construction
Juguete para Construir

Reversed grey angled plates that support the side walls are visible from the front of the structure.

The use of elements in four different colours produces a good approximation to the effect of the front of the Secretariat Building.

Joysticks find a new role as the flagpoles that line the front of the site.

Concealed grilles produce tiny holes on the facade of the Conference Building.

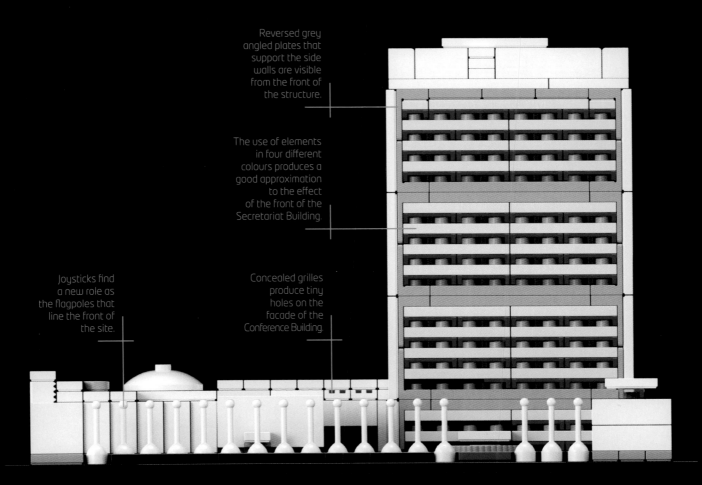

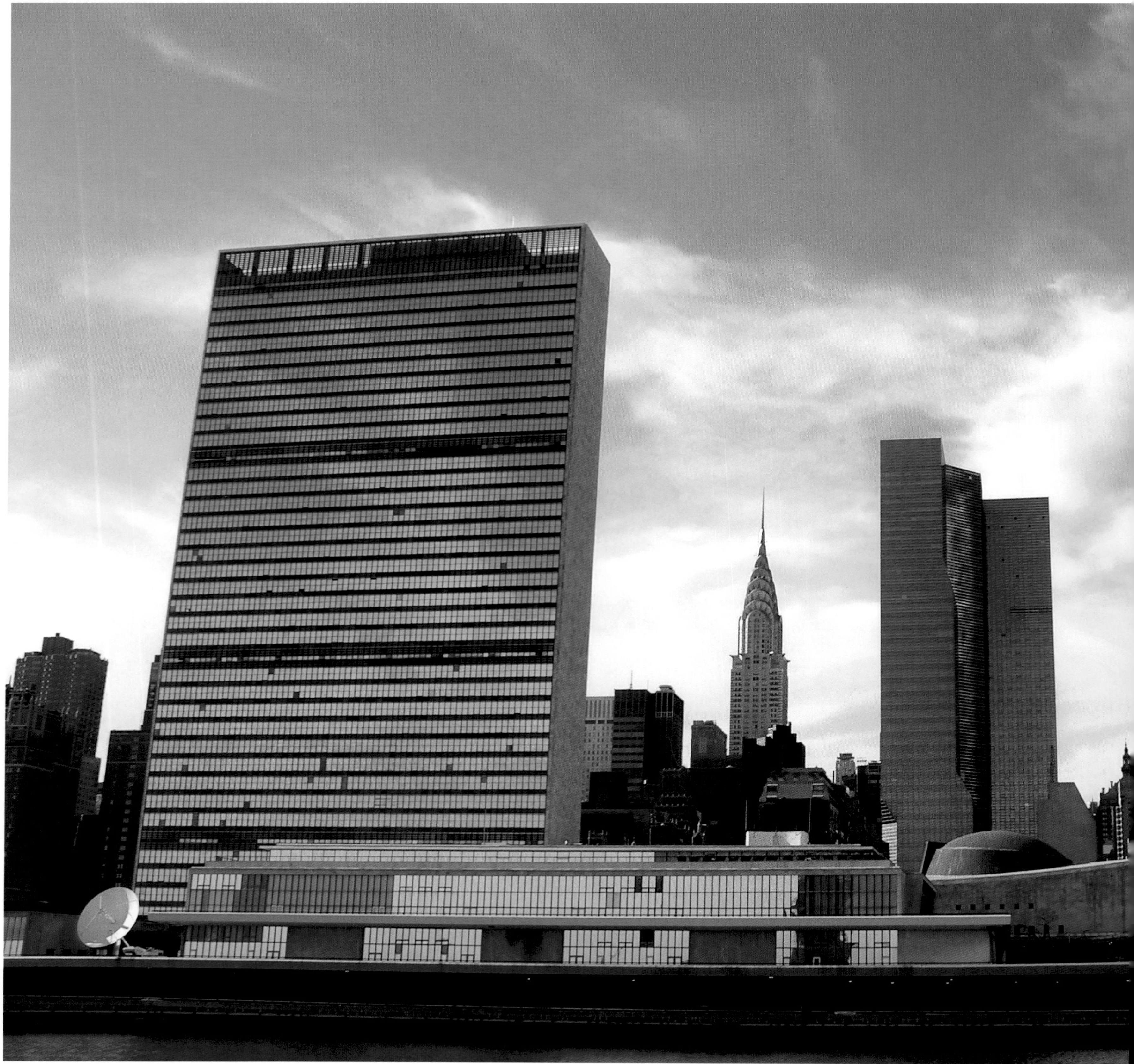

## Oscar Niemeyer
(1907–2012)
When he worked on the UN Headquarters, Niemeyer was the youngest member of the architectural panel. He became famous for his use of the sculptural qualities of building materials, especially concrete, and for his work on the planning and design of Brasilia, the capital of his native country.

**The Curtain Wall**
The main facade of the Secretariat Building is made up almost entirely of glass, with the structure of the building supported by a hidden framework within. The Secretariat was the first building in New York to have this type of glass curtain wall.

**A View from the River**
From the East River, the Secretariat Building towers over the site in the Turtle Bay district of Midtown Manhattan. In front is the curving river facade of the Conference Building, while the General Assembly Building, with its dome and upward turning wall resembling the hull of a great ship, is visible to the right.

# THE ORIGINAL

The story of the United Nations Headquarters began in the late 1940s, when the UN assembled a team of architects led by American Wallace K. Harrison to develop a design. The group came up with some 45 different plans, eventually settling on two, by Le Corbusier and Oscar Niemeyer, as the most promising. Whereas Le Corbusier intended to put the entire Headquarters into one large building, Niemeyer created a complex, with a large Secretariat tower and separate structures for the General Assembly Building, Conference Building, and Library. Niemeyer's scheme was chosen, although Le Corbusier advised on the positioning of the Secretariat Building.

Niemeyer's design is admired for the way it combines the dominant modernist tower with its more organic neighbours, with their curved concrete facades. The 39-storey Secretariat tower has become an internationally-recognised symbol of the UN, its green glass facade fronted by the row of flagpoles familiar from countless news broadcasts. The low-rise buildings are arranged carefully around the tower, their curved walls and the dome of the General Assembly Building looking like vast modernist sculptures.

# THE EIFFEL TOWER

## Capturing the Design

The Eiffel Tower is composed of an intricate network of iron bricks, and the LEGO® model cannot reproduce these at its small scale. Instead, the grey bricks combine to produce an abstract impression of the tower's overall form. The model therefore concentrates on capturing the design of the structure's key parts – the four converging legs, the various platforms, and the sweeping arches – using grey bricks to recall the colour of the original ironwork.

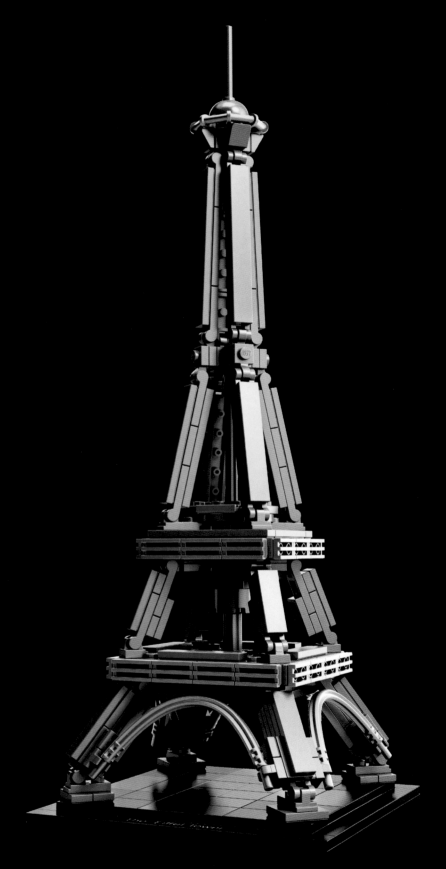

# THE EIFFEL TOWER

## LEGO® Artist: Rok Zgalin Kobe

The tallest and most iconic building in Paris, the Eiffel Tower was far from easy to model in LEGO® bricks. LEGO artist Rok Zgalin Kobe and builder Jørn Kristian Thomsen collaborated closely on the design of the model, and found several aspects of the project challenging. The way in which the four legs of the tower are angled inwards, the tapering structure of the tower's ironwork, the arches near ground level, and the design of the top of the structure all posed difficulties. One key to the model was to use LEGO parts that are designed to move, such as hinges and turntable bricks, to create the unusual angles and tapering shapes that were required. However, this produced another challenge – how to stabilise a structure built up using movable parts. The finished model, though, combines stability with a credible recreation of the tower's unique shape. In achieving this, the designers were helped not only by their own ingenuity and the rich repertoire of LEGO bricks, but also by the fame of the tower itself, which makes its striking shape instantly recognisable.

The tower's ironwork makes a striking contrast with the stone of the nearby houses

**Building** Eiffel Tower
**Engineers** Gustave Eiffel, Maurice Koechlin, Emile Nouguier, architect, Stephen Sauvestre
**Location** Paris, France
**Building type** Landmark tower

**Year** 1887-1889
**Construction type** Iron framework on stone bases
**Height** 324 m
**Square footage** 168,186 sq ft

*"The model of the Eiffel Tower involved many structural challenges that were solved as a result of a close collaboration between LEGO artist and builder".*

**Rok Zgalin Kobe**

# THE MODEL

Once the designers had worked out the principle of building the angled parts of the tower using hinged LEGO bricks, they had to decide how to fit these together while also creating a tower with the right proportions. A key decision was to build up the legs in layers, with the hinged parts sandwiched between an inner plate and an outer tile. This not only gives the legs strength, but also recreates the bulk of the legs in three dimensions. In keeping with the overall appearance of the real tower, there are more layers lower down, fewer higher up, so that the structure tapers. The arch at the bottom adds to the structure's bulk lower down, enhancing this tapering effect. On the real tower, the arch is purely decorative, but in the model it does stabilise and strengthen the structure slightly.

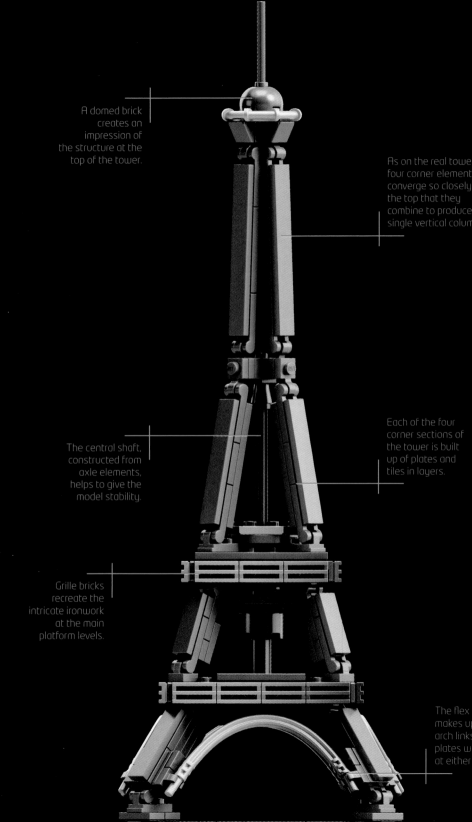

A domed brick creates an impression of the structure at the top of the tower.

As on the real tower four corner element converge so closely the top that they combine to produce single vertical colum

The central shaft, constructed from axle elements, helps to give the model stability.

Each of the four corner sections of the tower is built up of plates and tiles in layers.

Grille bricks recreate the intricate ironwork at the main platform levels.

The flex makes u arch links plates w at either

## Model 21019

The Eiffel Tower model has a deceptively small number of building steps because there are numerous sub-steps required to build each section of the tower before joining it to the main structure.

**LEGO artist** Rok Zgalin Kobe
**LEGO builder** Jørn Kristian Thomsen
**LEGO bricks** 321
**Building steps** 15
**Dimensions** 112 x 317 mm
**Release date** 2014

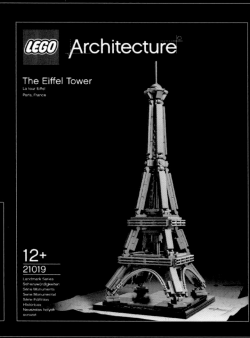

LEGO Architecture

The Eiffel Tower
La tour Eiffel
Paris, France

12+
21019

Landmark Series
Sehenswürdigkeiten
Série Monuments
Serie Monumental
Série Edifícios
Históricos
Nevezetes helyek
sorozat

The platforms are finished with smooth tile surfaces.

The arches bend gracefully to connect the tower's legs.

Grey and green tiles indicate the paving and grass areas around the base of the tower.

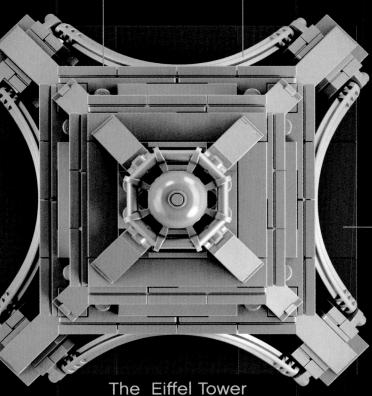

The Eiffel Tower

# IN FOCUS

Although the structure of the model is held together mainly by its numerous hinged bricks and linked to the base using four turntables, it has one other key element running through it. This is a central vertical column, which is an addition to the structure and is not present in the real Eiffel Tower. The column is made up of axles, some of which are linked by connectors. It does not run unbroken through the whole length of the model but is interrupted at the two main platform levels and anchored to them to give the structure rigidity. In the finished model the corner legs are so visually dominant that the central column fades into the background.

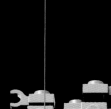

This rod produces the effect of the top of the tower and the antenna with which it is crowned

The upper platform of the structure is reduced to just this eight-sided parabolic ring

Grey slopes, like inverted buttresses, form the outer sides of the top platform

Fixing tiles holds together the structure of each of the upper sections of the tower

1x1 plates with horizontal clips form key elements of the hinges that enable the legs to be correctly positioned at an angle

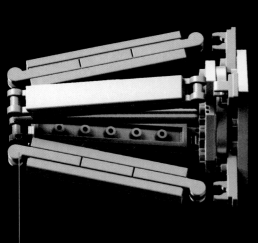
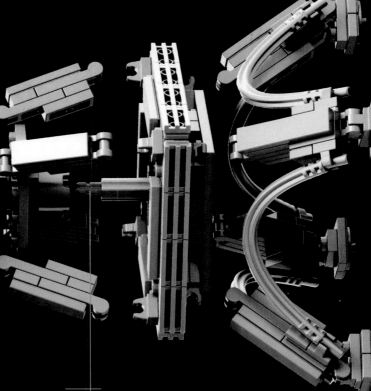

To allow the tower's connection to the base of the tower angle, each pair of legs has a pair of hinges plates fitted on to the upper part of turntable

Rows of outward facing grilles line the sides of the platforms, recreating the intricate ironwork.

1 x 2 plates with shafts form the other elements of the hinges; they are held securely between long tiles and plates

Axle-connectors are used to hold together the bricks of the central shaft

To attach the legs of the tower, the lower part of the turntable is fitted at each corner of the base.

**View from the Base**
Looking up the centre of the tower from ground level, the intricate latticework is clear. The numerous cross-braces make the tower strong while also keeping its weight relatively light.

# THE ORIGINAL

The Eiffel Tower was built for the 1889 Paris Exposition and was the brain-child of Maurice Koechlin and Emile Nouguier, two engineers who worked for French engineer and businessman Gustave Eiffel. Koechlin and Nouguier designed a simple and unadorned iron lattice tower, with four curving legs joined by horizontal girders. The design did not impress Eiffel, so he brought in architect Stephen Savestre, to improve the design. Savestre added arches, improved the first platform and made the ironwork more decorative. Eiffel liked the result and construction began in 1887. Built of prefabricated parts,

Eiffel's engineers took great care with the tower's specifications. Rivet holes were specified to an accuracy of within 0.1mm, to ensure that all the parts fitted together exactly. When the Exposition opened, thousands climbed 1,710 steps to the upper platform to enjoy the view. The tower was an instant success and visitor levels increased when the lift was installed. For 41 years the tower was world's tallest human-made structure and the skill of its engineers and the workers who put it together was widely admired. It soon became the universally recognised symbol of the city that it remains today.

**In the Champ de Mars**
The Eiffel Tower is set at the northwestern end of the Champ de Mars, a long public park in the centre of Paris. The trees and acres of grass of the Champ de Mars give the tower one of the best settings of any of the world's great structures.

# TREVI FOUNTAIN

### The Two Elements

The Trevi model is unusual in the LEGO®
Architecture series because it recreates not
a whole building but two separate elements
– the front of a building with the adjoining
statues and fountain. The model's use of colour,
however, and the way in which the fountain is
framed by a curving white wall that matches the
architecture behind, produces a unified effect that
enables the model to form a convincing whole.

Trevi Fountain

# TREVI FOUNTAIN

**LEGO® Artist: Rok Zgalin Kobe**

One of the most famous fountains in the world, the beautiful Trevi Fountain stands at the meeting of three roads, in front of a Baroque palace in the center of Rome. This landmark presented the LEGO® designer with unique challenges, namely how to recreate its two prominent features – the Baroque curves that the structure contains and the intricately carved sculptures – and other decorations that form such an important part of the fountain and palace facade. There is also the issue that a fountain is a moving object, and the LEGO model had to find a way of freezing the movement of the water while still suggesting it. A key solution was to define the structure using bricks of three colours – white for the main parts of the palace front and the statues attached to it; grey for the carved reliefs and the sculptures in the water; and blue for the windows and the water itself. The sculptures are recreated using a mix of techniques – most are built up in an abstract way using a wide range of bricks, but the three large statues on the palace front are minifigures – a unique feature for the LEGO Architecture series. This combination of abstract and more literal recreation is a successful blend that reflects the variety of the actual building and its dramatic Baroque style of architecture and carving.

Both palace and fountain are finished in warm, cream-colored stone.

**Building** Trevi Fountain
**Architect** Nicola Salvi (with Pietro Bracci and Luigi Vanvitelli)
**Location** Rome, Italy
**Building type** Fountain plus palace facade

**Year** 1732-1762
**Construction type** Solid carved stone
**Height** 26 m
**Width** 161 ft
**Architecture style** Baroque

*"Although the real fountain is very monochromatic, I chose to make the model using three colors, to help distinguish the features on the fountain and facade".*

**Rok Zgalin Kobe**

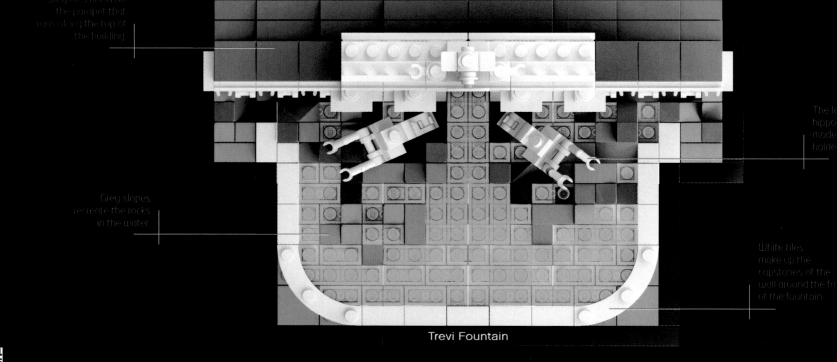

...the parapet that runs along the top of the building.

The l... hippo... mode... holde...

Grey slopes recreate the rocks in the water.

White tiles make up the capstones of the wall around the fr... of the fountain.

Trevi Fountain

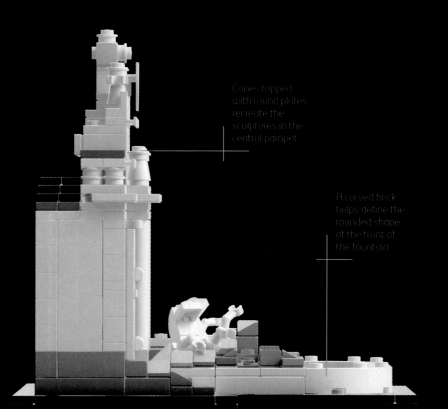

Cones topped with round plates recreate the sculptures in the central parapet

A curved brick helps define the rounded shape of the front of the fountain

# THE MODEL

LEGO artist Rok Zgalin Kobe wanted to avoid the palace facade looking dull and sought to create the sense of an interior behind the wall. To do this, and to give a sense of light shining out of the windows from inside the palace, he placed blue transparent bricks behind the windows. This makes the model feel deeper than it is, as well as giving a sense of colour harmony with the water of the fountain its...

Suggesting the intricate details of the facade required the ingenious use of LEGO bricks includin... plates with bars and plates with clips. These smal... bricks are contrasted with much larger elements – long white tiles to suggest vertical pilasters, and t... round bricks with square bases to suggest the lar... columns on either side of the central arch. The res... is a model almost as intricate as the architecture ... the original structure.

## Model 21020

The Trevi Fountain is an intricate model with a large number of elements, including many small bricks. More than 100 building steps are required to recreate the fountain's sculptures and the palace face.

**LEGO artist** Rok Žgalin Kobe
**LEGO builder** Jørn Kristian Thomsen
**LEGO bricks** 725
**Building steps** 102
**Dimensions** 208 x 143 mm
**Release date** 20

**LEGO Architecture**

Trevi Fountain
Fontana di Trevi
Rome, Italy

12+
21020

Landmark Series
Sehenswürdigkeiten
Série Monuments
Serie Monumental
Série Edifícios Históricos
Nevezetes helyek sorozat
Serie Landmark

Model designed by
Rok Žgalin Kobe

Transparent bricks, with transparent blue bricks behind, give a distinctive tint to the windows.

1x1 plates with horizontal clips form the capitals at the top of the pilasters.

Plates with handled bars realise the tiny balconies in front of the windows.

The heads of the hippocamps are made from a brick with arch element.

Trevi Fountain

**Oceanus**

The central statue of Oceanus shows the god standing on his shell-like chariot and looking down at one of the sea horses that he and the Tritons are taming. The statue, which fits perfectly in its niche in the palace front, was carved by Bracci.

# THE ORIGINAL

**Combined Effects**

While Salvi designed the fountain, his pupil and colleague Luigi Vanvitelli redesigned the palace facade so that its walls and tall pilasters of travertine beautifully match the marble statuary in front of it. Salvi died before the fountain and statuary were finished, and the sculptor Pietro Bracci saw to the completion of the work.

The Trevi Fountain is in Trevi Square in the Quirinale district of Rome. It marks the place where one of the ancient aqueducts, which brought water into the city, terminated. Over the years several popes had commissioned fountains in the city and in 1730, Pope Clement XII organised a competition to design a fountain in Trevi Square. Although he was not declared the outright winner of the competition, the architect Nicola Salvi was eventually awarded the commission.

Salvi designed the fountain around the theme of the taming of the oceans. The god Oceanus stands at the centre of the palace facade on his chariot, which is guided by two sea gods called Tritons. He is in the process of taming a pair of sea horses, or hippocamps. Other deities, including Hygieia, goddess of health and Copia, goddess of abundance, look on. The sculptures look particularly dramatic against the backdrop of the Palazzo Poli behind, which was remodelled to match the fountain and contains carved reliefs telling the story of the Roman aqueducts. Palace and fountain combine to create one of the most striking and effective landmarks in Rome.

# JOHN HANCOCK CENTER

172

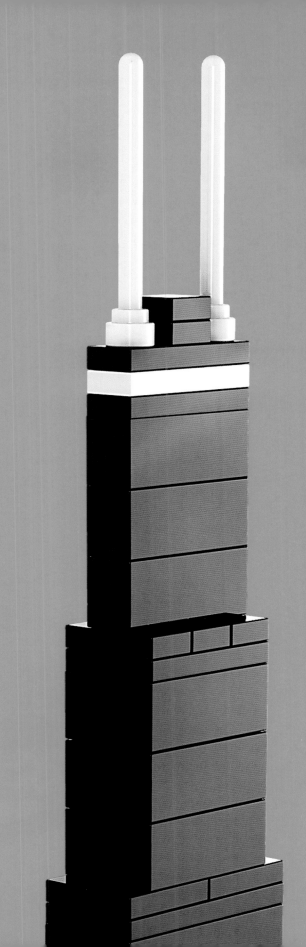

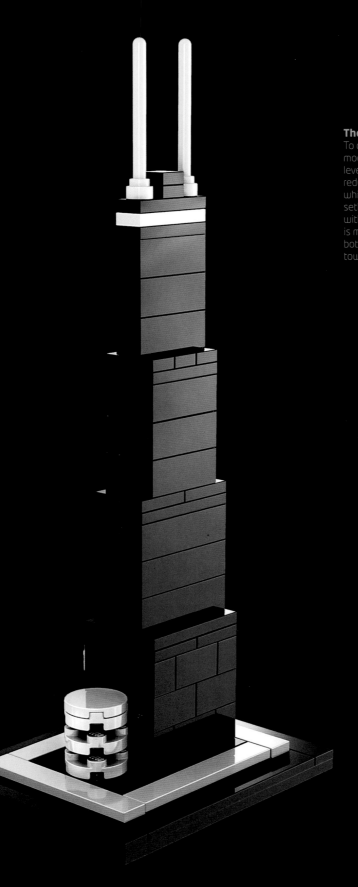

## The Tapering Tower

To create a sense of the building's taper, the model's setbacks work differently at different levels. The lowest and uppermost setbacks reduce the depth of the building by a single stud while keeping the breadth the same. The central setback works across the breadth of the tower without changing the depth. The combined effect is more subtle than if each setback had reduced both dimensions, and creates a sense of the tower's gentle taper.

# JOHN HANCOCK CENTER

## LEGO® Artist: Adam Reed Tucker

Chicago's John Hancock Center is a 100-storey skyscraper containing a mix of offices, shops and apartments, together with a restaurant. It is a familiar Chicago landmark both because of its height and its striking dark colour. The building also stands out because of its unusual tapered form – unlike its many straight-sided neighbours it is an elongated truncated pyramid. The building's sloping sides are impossible to reproduce in LEGO® bricks, so Adam Reed Tucker decided to portray the building using a series of setbacks, so that the model tapers from 3x4 studs at the bottom to 1x3 at the roof level where the antennae are mounted. At the model's relatively small scale, this gives the impression of a tapering form that, combined with the colour of the black bricks and plates, makes it easily recognisable as the John Hancock Center.

The building stands out above the surrounding buildings in the Streeterville area of Chicago.

**Building** John Hancock Center
**Architect** Skidmore, Owings and Merrill (lead architect, Bruce Graham)
**Location** Chicago, Illinois, U.S.A.
**Building type** Mixed-use tower
**Year** 1965–1970

**Construction type** Steel framed tube including external braces
**Height** 456.8 m
**Square footage** 2,799,973 sq. ft
**Architecture style** Modernist (structural expressionist)

*"A series of alternating setbacks seemed to be the best way to recreate the tower's gradually tapering shape".*

# THE MODEL

When standing close to the John Hancock Center, visitors can see that the building has a very noticeable surface texture defined by structural beams, X-shaped cross braces and the divisions between the floors. This is not so obvious when the tower is seen from further away, and the model does not attempt to reproduce this pattern precisely. However, Adam Reed Tucker did take advantage of the joins between the bricks to create a pattern on the sides of the model. This gives the model a subtle texture that recalls the way in which the walls of the real building are patterned.

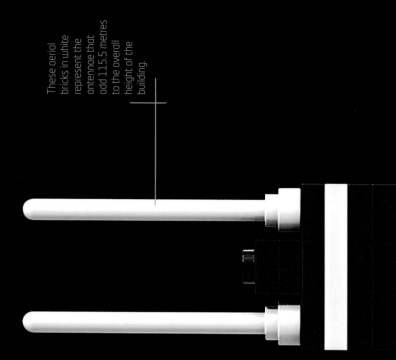

These aerial bricks in white represent the antenna that add 115.5 metres to the overall height of the building.

**LEGO** Architecture

## John Hancock Center
Chicago, Illinois, USA

Ages 10+
21001
Cont. 69 pcs
Construction model
Landmark series
designed by
Adam Reed Tucker
Booklet included
with details on
design and history

Building Toy

### Model 21001
Taking just 18 steps to build, the model captures the essence of the John Hancock Center, one of the most familiar modern buildings in Chicago.

**LEGO artist** Adam Reed Tucker
**LEGO builder** Steen Sig Andersen
**LEGO bricks** 69
**Building steps** 18
**Dimensions** 80 x 192 mm
**Release date** 2008

The joins between the bricks and tiles symbolise the surface of the tower, which in reality is broken up with numerous beams and cross-braces.

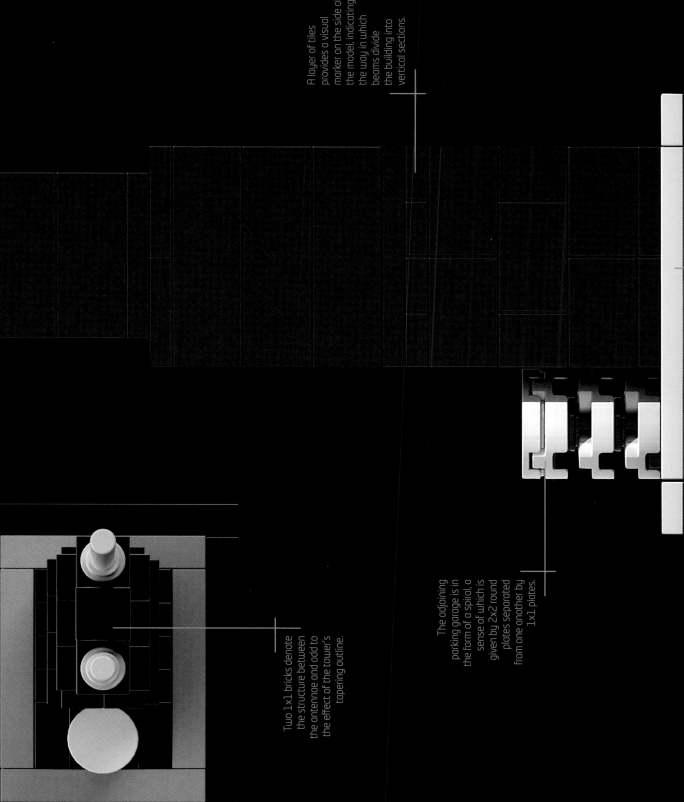

A layer of tiles provides a visual marker on the side of the model, indicating the way in which beams divide the building into vertical sections.

Two 1x1 bricks denote the structure between the antenna and add to the effect of the tower's tapering outline.

The adjoining parking garage is in the form of a spiral, a sense of which is given by 2x2 round plates separated from one another by 1x1 plates.

# IN FOCUS

Although dark finishes dominate the John Hancock Center – in both the real building and the model – there are a few paler highlights that set off the black surfaces, and these are recreated in the model. Chief among them are the pale antennae at the top of the building and the row of lights near the roof. In the real building, these lights change colour at different times of year (for example, they are set to shine green and red during the Christmas period). In the model they are kept white, although individual purchasers of the model may choose to customise them using their own coloured plates.

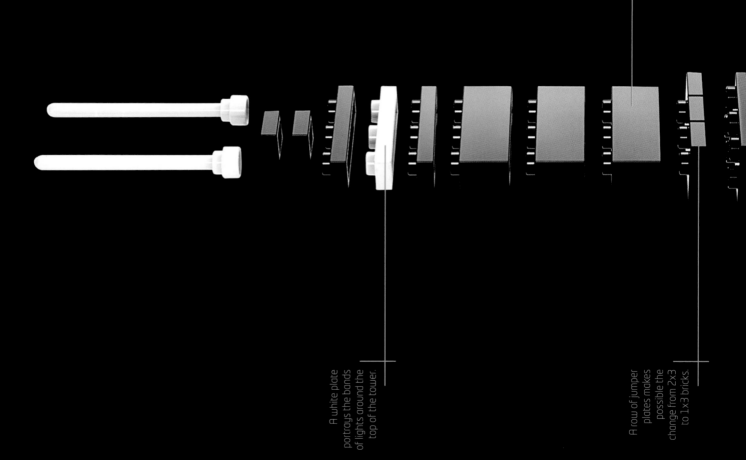

The transition to narrower bricks gives a sense of the tapering profile of the tower.

A white plate portrays the bands of lights around the top of the tower.

A row of jumper plates makes possible the change from 2x3 to 1x3 bricks.

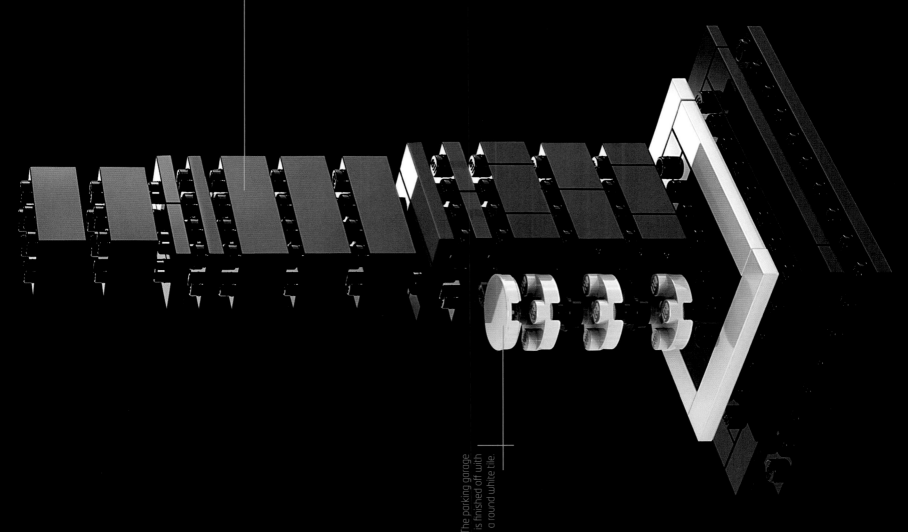

The shiny black surface of the bricks creates a similar impression to the way the tower looks when viewed from a distance, so that the model works at its small scale.

The parking garage is finished off with a round white tile.

**Steel on Show**
A vast amount of steel was required to produce the facade's columns and braces. Yet the innovative structure meant it could be built with half the steel necessary for a conventional internal-frame skyscraper.

# THE ORIGINAL

Traditional skyscrapers are supported by a steel frame hidden inside the building; their outer walls are like a skin concealing the inner skeleton. The John Hancock Center turned this idea inside-out. Engineer Fazlur Khan and architect Bruce Graham put key structural elements – upright columns and X-shaped braces – on the outside of the building, creating a structural tube that effectively carries the enormous force of the wind, as well as helping to support the vast building's weight. This approach also produced a building that looked different from any previous skyscraper, and the architect enhanced its appearance further by using black anodised aluminum for many of the finishes. When it was built, the John Hancock Center – with nearly 900,000 square feet of office space, 700 condominiums, and most of the facilities required to service them, including a supermarket and post office – was the world's tallest multi-use tower. Although its record has long been broken, it is still an architectural landmark with a unique and instantly recognisable design.

**The Skyscraper's Setting**
Set on the edge of downtown and on one of the city's key traffic arteries, the tower is one of the most prominent buildings on Chicago's "Magnificent Mile", the section of Michigan Avenue that is home to exclusive shops, high-end hotels, and major office buildings.

# WILLIS TOWER

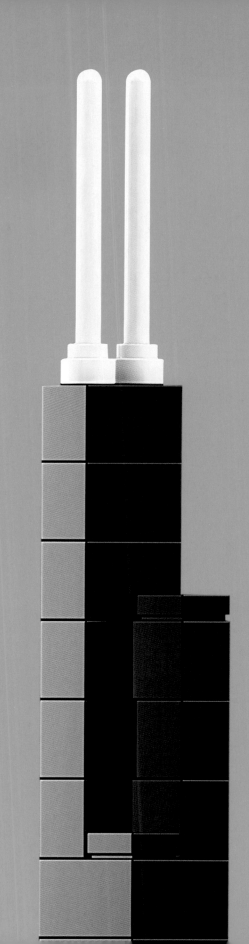

## The Scale of the Model

The LEGO® model of the Willis Building is at quite a small scale – it portrays the vast structure in a form that is just 18 bricks high. However, the LEGO artist Adam Reed Tucker took care to recreate the proportions of the tower's nine separate tubes, so that the stepped-back appearance of the upper portion of the building is obvious.

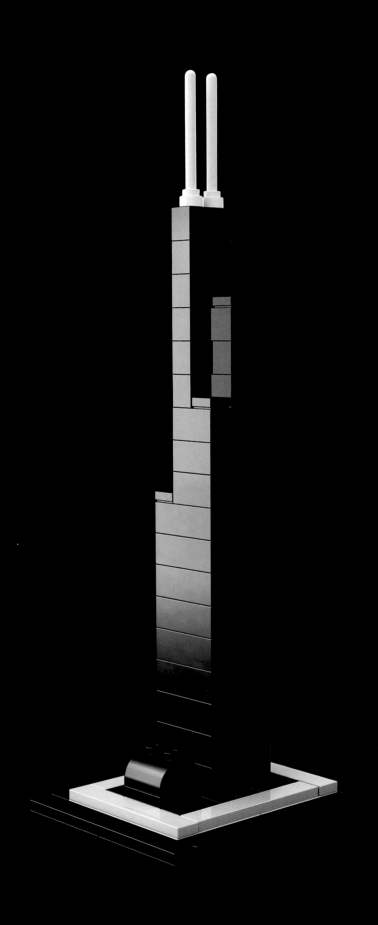

# WILLIS TOWER

**LEGO® Artist: Adam Reed Tucker**

When it was completed in 1974, Chicago's Willis Tower (originally named the Sears Tower) was the world's tallest building. Although it lost this record in 1998, the tower is still well known, not just for its sheer size but for its innovative structure. It is made up of what are in effect nine separate buildings, of various different heights, bundled together. Willis Tower is the earliest example of this type of construction, which is known as the bundled tube and was the invention of the engineer Fazlur Khan, who worked on the building with architects Skidmore, Owings and Merrill. The LEGO® model clearly portrays these separate tubes, each of which is 1x1 stud in size. The tubes rise to different heights and just two of them extend to the full height of the tower, providing two studs at the top to attach the tall white antennae, which are such a striking feature of the building.

Separate vertical elements stand out clearly when the tower is viewed from one corner.

**Building** Willis Tower
**Architect** Skidmore, Owings and Merrill (lead architect, Bruce Graham)
**Location** Chicago, Illinois, U.S.A.
**Building type** Office tower

**Year** 1970–1974
**Construction type** Steel frame and curtain walls (bundled tube)
**Height** 441.96 m
**Square footage** 4,477,800 sq. ft
**Architecture style** International style

*"The aim was to recreate the nine bundled tubes of the tower, and I decided to do this by using a 1x1 model and building straight up"*

# THE MODEL

The Willis Tower's steel structure is faced in black aluminium. This material, together with the rows of bronze-tinted glass windows, makes the skyscraper look dark, especially when viewed from a distance. Adam Reed Tucker therefore used black LEGO bricks for almost the entire model. The apparent colour of the bricks varies according to the light, creating a similar effect to the way in which the real building looks different depending on the time of day or the weather. Although the scale of the model is small, it is large enough to include the entrance building on Upper Wacker Drive – a spacious structure that has a height equivalent to several storeys of the main tower. This structure has a metal frame and is almost completely glazed. A bowed brick was the ideal brick to represent its barrel-vaulted structure.

These white bricks are ideal for the tall antennae on top of the building, which stand out against the dark colours of the rest of the structure.

Joins between the bricks create the impression of the pattern of horizontals running up the tower.

x2 brick with s represents the entrance uilding at the f the tower.

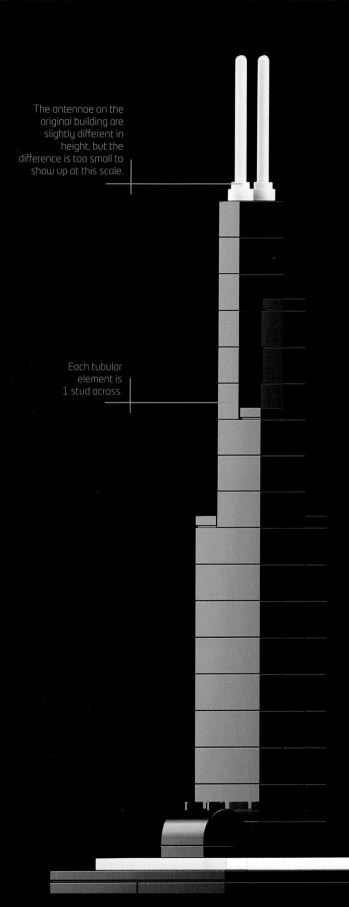

The antennae on the original building are slightly different in height, but the difference is too small to show up at this scale.

Each tubular element is 1 stud across.

White tiles line the base of the model, helping to set off the dark tower and balance the white of the antennae.

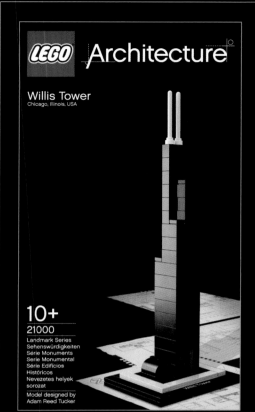

**Model 21000**
The shiny black model catche the light well so that the joins between the bricks, symbolizi the horizontal divisions in the building, appear as dark lines.

**LEGO artist** Adam Reed Tucker
**LEGO builder** Steen Sig Andersen
**LEGO bricks** 69
**Building steps** 17
**Dimensions** 80 x 228 m
**Release dates** 2008 and 2011

---

### LEGO Architecture

**Willis Tower**
Chicago, Illinois, USA

10+
21000

Landmark Series
Sehenswürdigkeiten
Série Monuments
Serie Monumental
Série Edifícios Históricos
Nevezetes helyek sorozat

Model designed by
Adam Reed Tucker

# IN FOCUS

Once the artist had decided on the model's dimensions, making it work was mainly a question of building upwards so that each of the nine bundled tubes reached the right height in relation to its neighbours. This was more than just fitting one brick on top of another, however. The bricks are carefully interlocked so that the model has sufficient strength all the way up. This involves alternating the positions of the two sizes of brick used in the lower half of the tower, and the use of 1x3 LEGO bricks in the upper section, to tie the tubes together. By using bricks almost exclusively, Adam Reed Tucker was able to create a rhythm of horizontals all the way up the tower. Although there are far fewer horizontal lines than on the original building, these joins still help to produce the effect of a tower with regular horizontal bands.

A single 1x1 tile tops each tubular element of the tower.

The length of the antennae bricks was one factor that helped to determine the overall scale of the model.

1x3 bricks bridge the 1x1 bricks below, strengthening the structure of this part of the model.

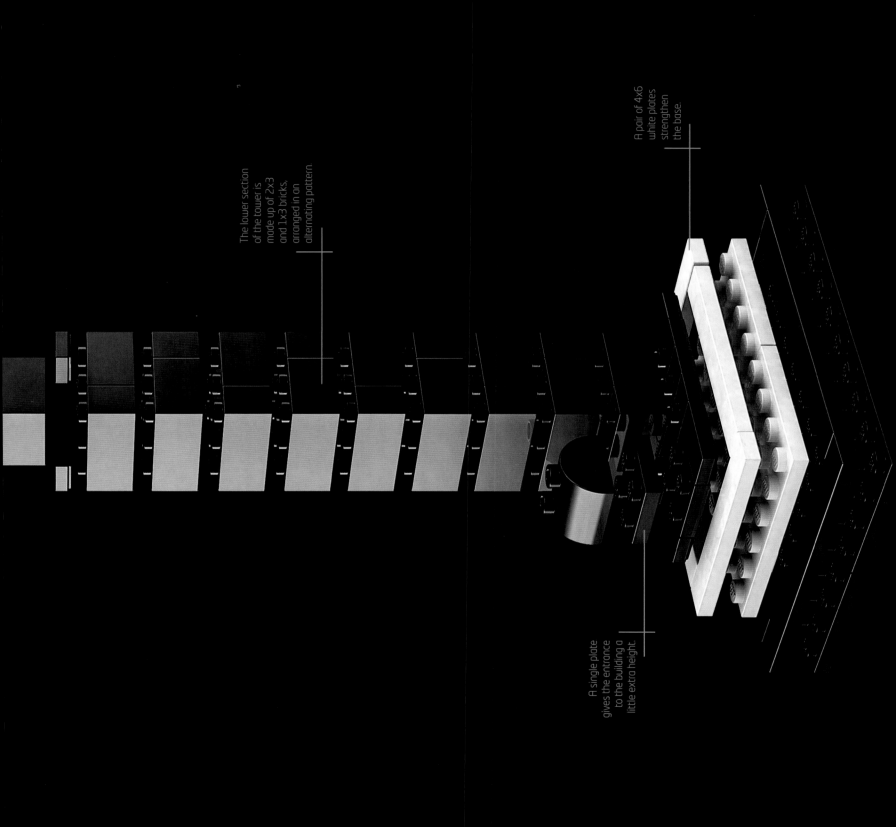

The lower section of the tower is made up of 2x3 and 1x3 bricks, arranged in an alternating pattern.

A pair of 4x6 white plates strengthen the base.

A single plate gives the entrance to the building a little extra height.

# THE ORIGINAL

When Sears, Roebuck & Co., then the world's largest retailer, commissioned the tower (originally named Sears Tower) in 1969 to house their offices, they wanted a tall, landmark building with plenty of uninterrupted floor space. This was one reason why the architect and engineer adopted the tube system for the tower's structure – it puts the main structural beams and uprights on the outside of each vertical section, leaving internal floors uncluttered. The tube design also made it possible to heighten some parts of the building in the future, if the owners required further space.

This kind of structure has another key advantage: the strong outer walls withstand wind particularly well, and nowhere is wind load a more important consideration than in the famously windy city of Chicago. The way in which the tower's profile diminishes as it gets higher also helps reduce the wind load towards the top.

In 1994, Sears sold the building, and since then it has had various occupants. One of these, insurance company Willis Group, won the right to rename the tower when they leased part of it in 2009.

**A Heavyweight on the Skyline**
Viewed across Lake Michigan, the Willis Tower's 16,000 windows glow with light. The enormous structure weighs some 222,500 tonnes and is supported by 114 piles in the ground beneath.

# EMPIRE STATE BUILDING

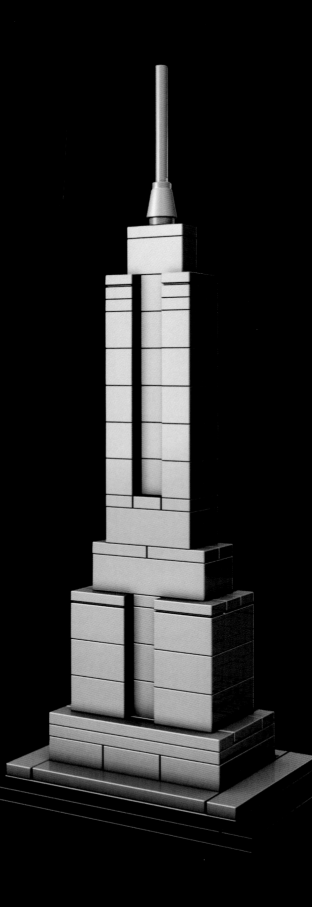

# EMPIRE STATE BUILDING

**LEGO® Artist: Adam Reed Tucker**

When it was completed in 1931, New York City's Empire State Building was the tallest skyscraper in the world for nearly 40 years. The tower remains one of the world's most iconic buildings – because it was the first skyscraper to have more than 100 floors, because it is a prime example of the Art Deco style and because it is a powerful symbol of the U.S.A.'s recovery from the Great Depression. To make an effective LEGO® model of this celebrated building, which still towers above its Manhattan neighburs, Adam Reed Tucker concentrated on the Empire State Building's Art Deco lines, using a series of setbacks to recreate the skyscraper's well known shape as it rises from its broad base to its tall, slender spire. The result is a clear example of the way that a simple model, made with a small number of bricks, can cature the essence of one of the world's largest and most familiar structures.

The skyscraper rises high above the surrounding streets of Midtown Manhattan.

**Building** Empire State Building
**Architect** Shreve, Lamb & Hudson
**Location** New York City, U.S.A.
**Building type** Office block (with retail and corporate tenants, broadcast antenna, and Observatory)

**Year** 1930-1931
**Construction type** Steel frame with limestone cladding
**Height** 439.9 m (to top of antenna)
**Square footage** 2.85 million rentable sq. ft
**Architecture style** Art Deco

*"The challenge was to simplify the building down to its basic profile. The result was very different from the one-off 8-foot-tall model of the Empire State Building I built when I started to make LEGO models of real buildings".*

**Adam Reed Tucker**

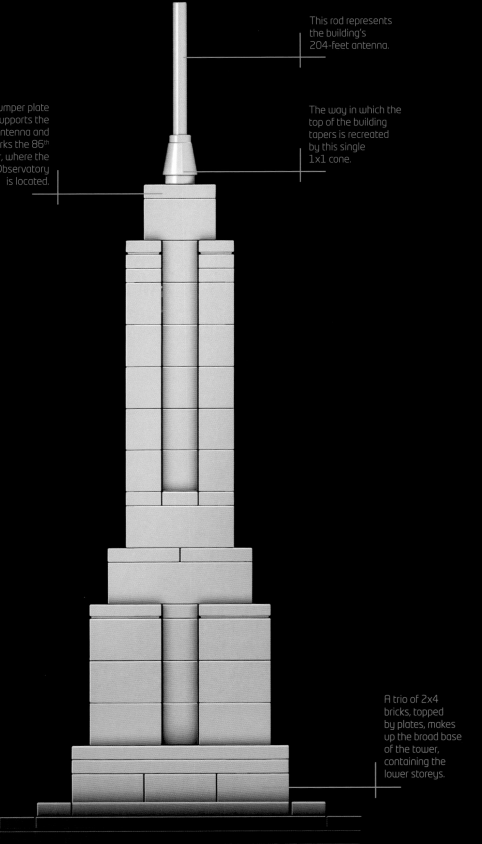

This rod represents the building's 204-feet antenna.

A jumper plate supports the antenna and marks the 86th floor, where the Observatory is located.

The way in which the top of the building tapers is recreated by this single 1x1 cone.

# THE MODE

One of the most important aspects of th is the way in which it creates the effect Empire State's Art Deco architecture by few subtle variations in the sizes and arr of the LEGO bricks. The model's slender pointed top are true to the narrow, upwo pointing shape of the skyscraper, but th also includes horizontal lines, especially at the top of each vertical section. The r recreates some of these by including pla or tiles at the top of each vertical sectio The placing of these plates and tiles pro an effect that is faithful both to the origi building and the Art Deco style in genera

There are offsets all around the model, most of which reduce the size of each side by just half a stud.

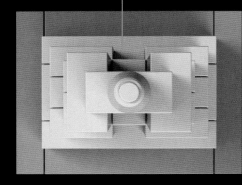

A trio of 2x4 bricks, topped by plates, makes up the broad base of the tower, containing the lower storeys.

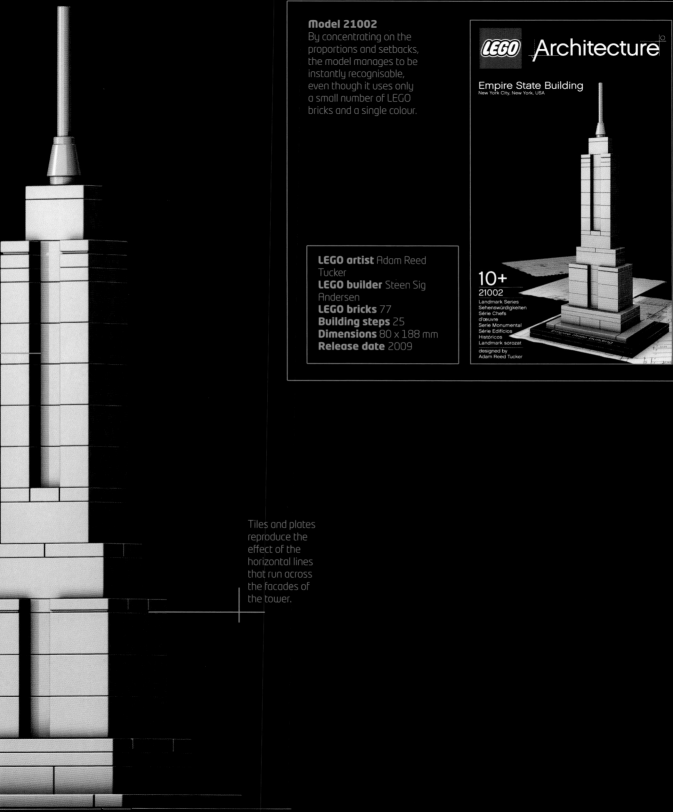

## Model 21002

By concentrating on the proportions and setbacks, the model manages to be instantly recognisable, even though it uses only a small number of LEGO bricks and a single colour.

**LEGO artist** Adam Reed Tucker
**LEGO builder** Steen Sig Andersen
**LEGO bricks** 77
**Building steps** 25
**Dimensions** 80 x 188 mm
**Release date** 2009

**LEGO** Architecture

### Empire State Building
New York City, New York, USA

10+

21002

Landmark Series
Sehenswürdigkeiten
Série Chefs
d'œuvre
Serie Monumental
Série Edifícios
Históricos
Landmark sorozat

designed by
Adam Reed Tucker

Tiles and plates reproduce the effect of the horizontal lines that run across the facades of the tower.

# IN FOCUS

One of the challenges with the Empire State Building model was keeping the structure sound. The reason for this is the way in which parts of the tower are built up using bricks of the same size placed one on top of another without any overlap or side connections to link them together. To prevent this from weakening the structure, the artist bridged the lower sections with a 2x4 brick, joining them together firmly. Higher up the tower, there was a similar issue, but with the much smaller bricks used here, no chance of bridging them with a large brick. The artist therefore used a brick with a side pin, linked to a brick with a hole, to make a horizontal join and add structural integrity. Thus the finished model is very strong, in spite of the fact that it is both tall and slender.

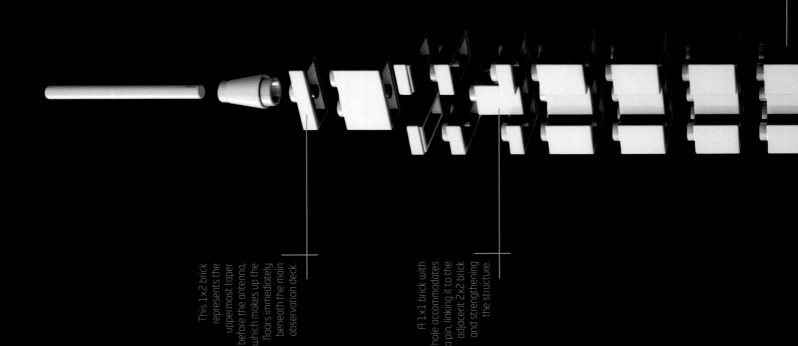

This 1x2 brick represents the uppermost taper before the antenna, which makes up the floors immediately beneath the main observation deck.

A 1x1 brick with a hole accommodates a pin, linking it to the adjacent 2x2 brick and strengthening the structure.

The main upper part of the tower is built from 1x2 and 1x1 bricks laid side by side and not linked together.

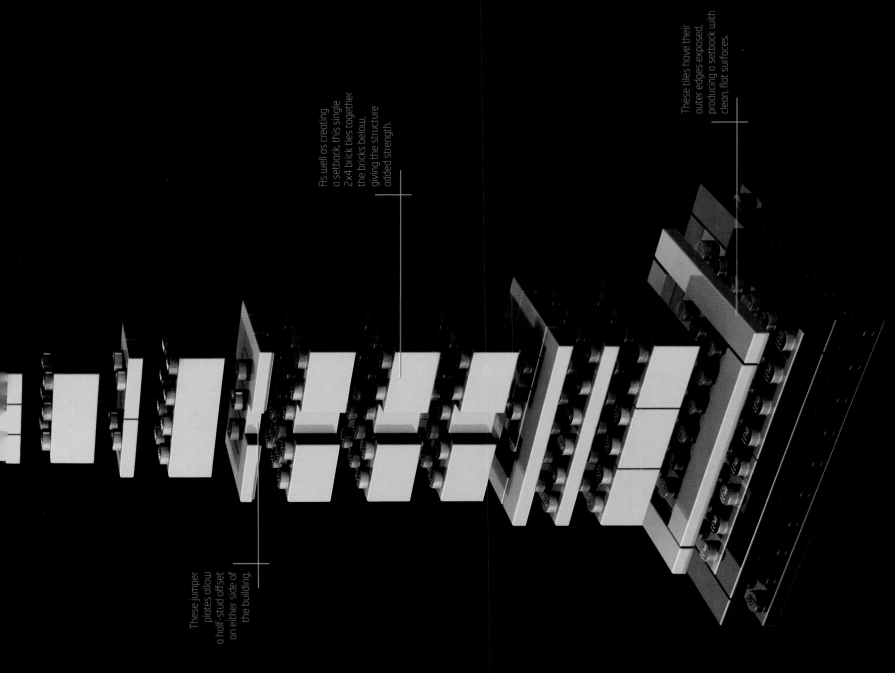

These tiles have their outer edges exposed, producing a setback with clean, flat surfaces.

As well as creating a setback, this single 2x4 brick ties together the bricks below, giving the structure added strength.

These jumper plates allow a half-stud offset on either side of the building.

**View from Above**
The intricate structure of the Empire State Building's antenna, with its corner buttresses and circular spire, is only clearly visible when the tower is seen from the air.

# THE ORIGINAL

The story of the Empire State Building began when the owner of the site, John Jacob Raskob, approached architect William Lamb of the firm Shreve, Lamb and Harmon. Raskob is said to have stood a pencil on the eraser end and asked Lamb, "How tall can you make it without it falling down?" Lamb's design evolved rapidly, as a series of setbacks culminating in a slender antenna – a perfect example of the ever-fashionable Art Deco style. Lamb and his engineers devised a steel frame structure with the elevators in a central core, and offices around the edge of each floor. This kind of frame structure enabled the builders to work quickly, using a vast workforce made possible by low labour costs during the Great Depression. The groundbreaking took place on 17 March 1930, and the building was opened on 1 May 1931. The architect and builders had brought off a triumph – the building's height and elegant design made it a hit with the public, and it kept its height record until the World Trade Center's North Tower was completed in 1970.

**Towering Over Manhattan and Beyond**
The Empire State Building once dwarfed its neighbours. Though there are now other tall buildings in the area, it still dominates the skyline. On a clear day, visitors can see five states from the building's Observatories.

# SEATTLE SPACE NEEDLE

**Reaching for the Sky**
The designers of the Space Needle were keen to
build a tall landmark that would dominate the city
skyline and pinpoint the site of the World's Fair.
The LEGO® model's slender curving braces and
long central column help to create the impression
of just such a tall and upward-pointing structure.
The crowning antenna component also adds to
this impression. It is actually proportionally taller
and narrower than the topmost part of the real
building, but works well in the model to create
a sense of the overall form of the Space Needle.

# SEATTLE SPACE NEEDLE

### LEGO® Artist: Adam Reed Tucker

The Seattle Space Needle is a landmark tower that was built for the 1962 World's Fair. At the time it was the tallest building west of the Mississippi, and the futuristic structure soon became famous as a symbol of its home city. Tall, slender and full of circles and curves, the Space Needle does not look like the kind of landmark that would be easy to recreate using LEGO® bricks. However, the LEGO model succeeds because artist Adam Reed Tucker adopted some lateral thinking, using bricks not normally seen in the Architecture series and orienting them differently from normal. By using a number of LEGO® Technic bricks, the artist not only produced a recognisable recreation of the landmark structure, but also created a model that is true to the consciously modern and high-tech spirit of the original building.

The building's supporting legs take double form, but still give an impression of lightness.

**Building** Seattle Space Needle
**Architect** John Graham, with Victor Steinbrueck
**Location** Seattle, Washington State, U.S.A.

**Building type** Observation tower
**Year** 1961–1962
**Construction type** Concrete and steel
**Height** 184.4 m
**Architecture style** Modernist

*"Like many of the other models in the Architecture series, the Space Needle shows how pieces intended for very different uses can be given new and interesting roles".*

**Adam Reed Tucker**

# LEGO Architecture

## Seattle Space Needle
Seattle, Washington, USA

Ages 10+
21003
Cont. 57 pcs
Construction model
Landmark series
1st edition
designed by
Adam Reed Tucker
Booklet included
with details on
design and history

### Model 21003
In terms of building steps, the Seattle Space Needle is one of the simplest models in the Architecture series. However, it still manages to portray many of the key features of this quite complex structure.

**LEGO artist** Adam Reed Tucker
**LEGO builder** Steen Sig Andersen
**LEGO bricks** 57
**Building steps** 19
**Dimensions** 80 x 228 mm
**Release date** 2009

# THE MODEL

The LEGO model of the Space Needle contains very few plates and tiles and no standard LEGO bricks at all. Its main elements were originally intended for completely different roles, mainly in LEGO Technic models. Gear wheels represent the strips of windows running around the structure; satellite dishes turn into shell-like roofs; the central upright is made of LEGO Technic axle elements and the three curved legs that run most of the height of the Space Needle and form such an important part of the structure are made from lengths of flexible tubing. This ingenious use of elements produces an effect that recreates the building's slender silhouette, its lightweight appearance, and a number of its key details.

A whip aerial element represents the part of the real building that contains the illuminating section and, at the very tip, the aircraft warning beacon.

The windows of the restaurant are symbolised by the teeth of a LEGO Technic gear wheel.

A small satellite dish portrays the structure of the uppermost storey, which contains equipment such as the elevator machinery.

A pair of bevel gears represent the Skyline Level, included in the original design but only added to the building in 1982, which houses banqueting facilities.

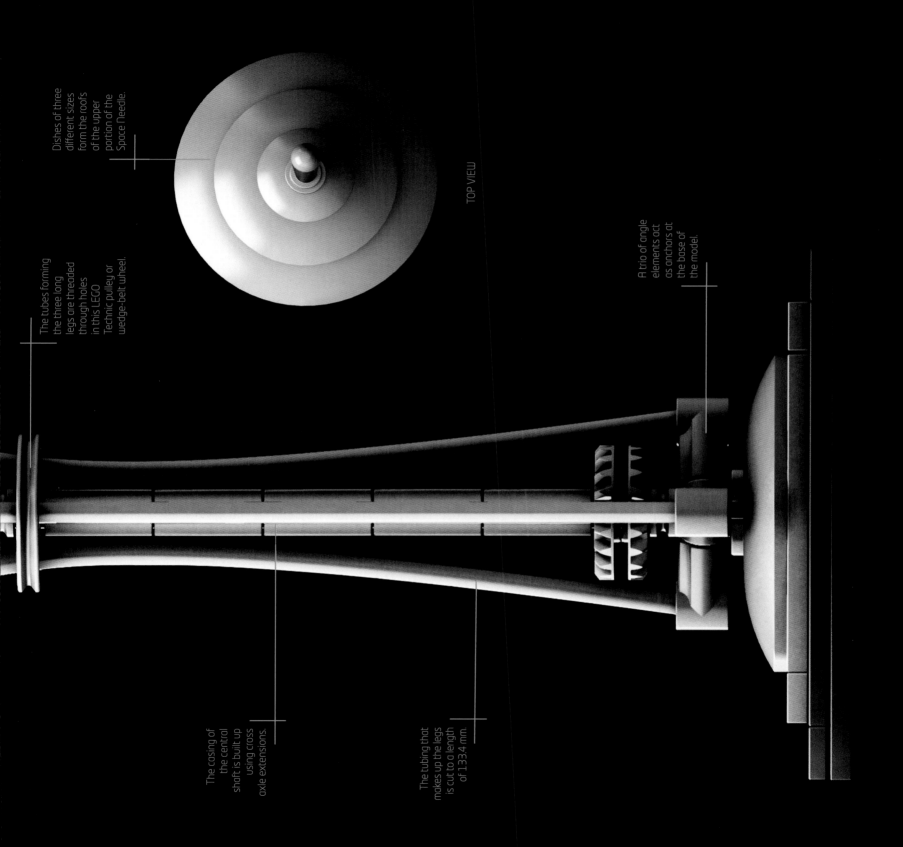

Dishes of three different sizes form the roofs of the upper portion of the Space Needle.

TOP VIEW

The tubes forming the three long legs are threaded through holes in this LEGO Technic pulley or wedge-belt wheel.

A trio of angle elements act as anchors at the base of the model.

The casing of the central shaft is built up using cross axle extensions.

The tubing that makes up the legs is cut to a length of 133.4 mm.

# IN FOCUS

Using LEGO Technic bricks enabled artist Adam Reed Tucker to take advantage of a method of construction using cross axles. But, instead of arranging them horizontally in the usual way, he used these axles in an upright position so that they form the spine of the model. These axle bricks, which run up the model's central column, are secured in cross-shaped holes in elements such as round bricks, gear wheels and a pulley (or wedge-belt wheel) to give the model structural rigidity. This method of construction lends itself to the circular shape of many of the parts of the tower and blends well visually with other elements that are round but cannot be attached directly to the axles, such as the satellite dishes.

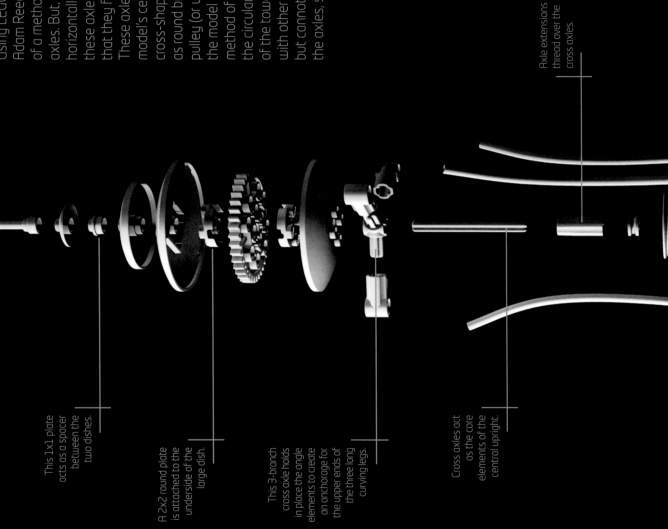

This 1x1 plate acts as a spacer between the two dishes.

A 2x2 round plate is attached to the underside of the large dish.

This 3-branch cross axle holds in place the angle elements to create an anchorage for the upper ends of the three long curving legs.

Cross axles act as the core elements of the central upright.

Axle extensions thread over the cross axles.

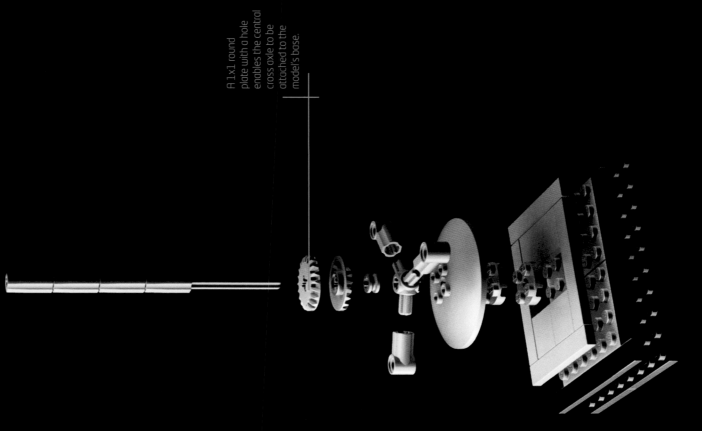

A 1x1 round plate with a hole enables the central cross axle to be attached to the model's base.

**John Graham Jr.**
(1908–1991)
Graham was a partner with his English-born father, also called John, in the Seattle architecture firm John Graham and Associates. They designed a number of important buildings in Seattle, as well as landmark modernist office towers in cities such as San Francisco and Rochester, New York. Another Seattle architect, Victor Steinbrueck, was consultant on the Space Needle and contributed to its design.

**The View from Below**
Looking up from ground level, the eye-catching ribbed underside of the restaurant stands out clearly.

# THE ORIGINAL

The Space Needle was originally part of the 1962 World's Fair, which Seattle businessman Edward E. Carlson was instrumental in bringing to his home city. During the run-up to the fair, Carlson did a quick sketch of a tower he wanted as its centerpiece. He envisaged a tall observation tower with a restaurant at the top, a structure similar to one built in Stuttgart, Germany, in the 1950s. The Space Needle's architect, John Graham, developed Carlson's idea, designing the restaurant like a flying saucer, and supporting it on a trio of slender legs with a central shaft carrying elevators. To make the structure stable, Graham set it on a platform of concrete some 36.6 metres across and 9 metres deep.

The finished Space Needle was hugely popular, with almost 20,000 visitors per day during the Fair. In the 1960s, the structure seemed futuristic with its revolving restaurant. The Space Needle remains popular for its viewing platform, restaurant and banqueting venue.

**A Stunning Vista**
Illuminated at night, the Needle stands out among Seattle's straight-lined skyscrapers. The restaurant and observation floor in the flying-saucer-shaped pod are more than 183 m above the ground and give visitors an unrivalled view. For diners, this view changes continuously as the outer part of the restaurant floor slowly revolves.

# BURJ KHALIFA

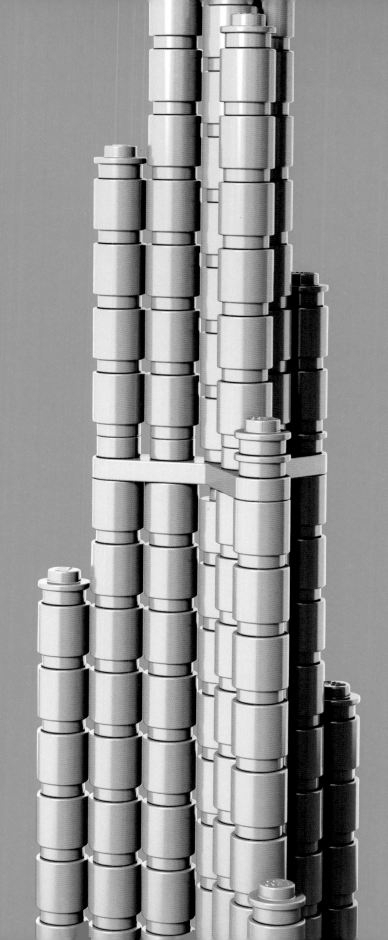

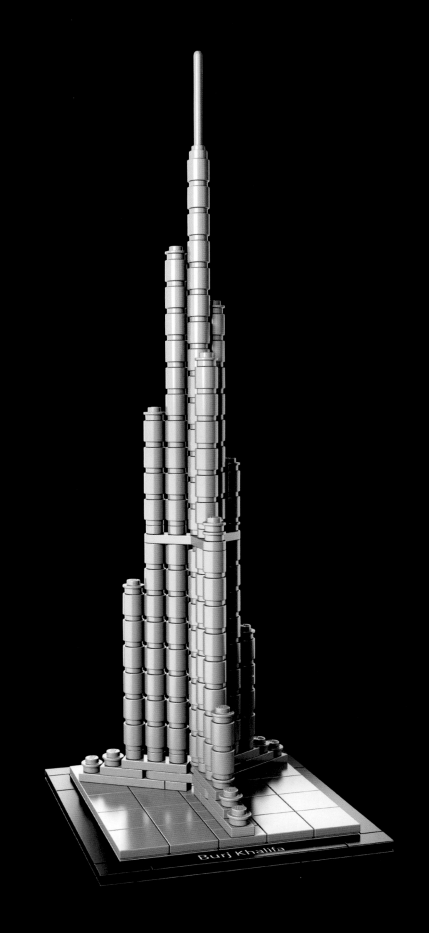

## Colour Versus Form

Apart from the black edge of the base, the model of Burj Khalifa consists entirely of grey bricks. Although these do not match exactly the mix of silver, grey and blue in the real structure, they create the impression of a building seen from a distance, when the separate colours become less easy to distinguish and the viewer's eye focuses on the overall form and shape of the building.

Burj Khalifa

# BURJ KHALIFA

## LEGO® Artist: Adam Reed Tucker

As the world's tallest building, Dubai's Burj Khalifa was an obvious choice for a LEGO® model that people all over the world would want to build. However, the tower's unique structure and form posed a problem from the outset for Adam Reed Tucker, the LEGO artist who created the model. Burj Khalifa is based on a Y-shaped, three-armed plan, involving angles that do not conform to the standard right-angled grid used in LEGO constructions. The model went through nine different versions during the design process, as the artist worked out how to support the tower on its base, how to form its rounded sections and how to build up the structure to the required height. The key to the model's construction was the LEGO® Technic three-blade rotor, which provided a basis for the Y-shaped geometry of the tower and is the heart of a base with three arms, each with three nodes plus a central node. The tower's ten main sections grow upwards from these points until the characteristic pointed shape of the building is complete.

Even in Dubai, a city of tall modern buildings, Burj Khalifa stands out.

**Building** Burj Khalifa
**Architect** Skidmore, Owings and Merrill (Adrian Smith)
**Location** Dubai, United Arab Emirates
**Building type** Mixed-use supertall tower (offices, apartments, hotel)
**Year** 2004–2010

**Construction type** Reinforced concrete and steel (bundled tube with buttressed core)
**Height** 829.7 m (to tip)
**Square footage** 5.67 million sq. ft
**Architecture style** Modern with elements influenced by Islamic architecture

*"The key decision was to build the model using stacked columns, cutting them off at different heights, to recreate the different setbacks that occur around the building".*

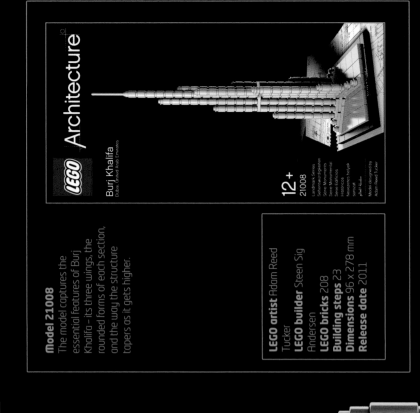

# LEGO Architecture

## Burj Khalifa
Dubai, United Arab Emirates

12+
21008

Landmark Series
Sehenswürdigkeiten
Serie Monumentos
Serie Edificios
Históricos
Nevezetes helyek
sorozat
سلسلة

Model designed by
Adam Reed Tucker

### Model 21008
The model captures the
essential features of Burj
Khalifa – its three wings, the
rounded forms of each section,
and the way the structure
tapers as it gets higher.

**LEGO artist** Adam Reed
Tucker
**LEGO builder** Steen Sig
Andersen
**LEGO bricks** 208
**Building steps** 23
**Dimensions** 96 x 278 mm
**Release date** 2011

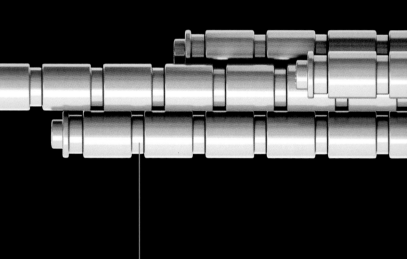

Each section is topped
with a 1x1 round plate,
to recreate the effect
of a roof.

TOP VIEW

The joins
between the
bricks recreate
the horizontal
banding around
the skyscraper.

# THE MODEL

The LEGO model of Burj Khalifa is very
simple in principle. It is made up mainly of 112
1x1 round bricks, their shape matching the
multiple bundled sections of the enormous tower.
However, the model also recreates several of
the skyscraper's key details, from the sprawling
lower levels to the slender, pointed top. These
elements make the overall shape of the model
convincing, as do the varying heights of the
sections. These differ hugely in size. Each of
the tower's three wings has five sections, two of
which form part of the building's low, sprawling
base and rise only 2 or 3 plates from the ground.
The other, tower-like sections of the building vary
from 2 to 22 LEGO bricks in height, reproducing
Burj Khalifa's distinctive, skyward-pointing profile.

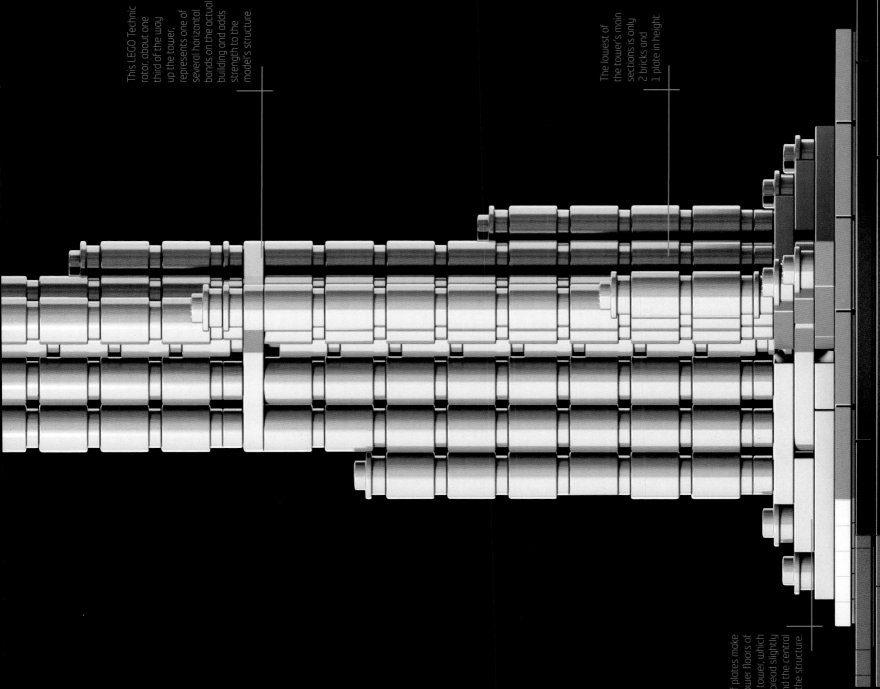

This LEGO Technic rotor, about one third of the way up the tower, represents one of several horizontal bands on the actual building and adds strength to the model's structure.

The lowest of the tower's main sections is only 2 bricks and 1 plate in height.

f plates make
wer floors of
tower, which
read slightly
nd the central
he structure.

# IN FOCUS

The unusual three-armed form of the tower, with each arm set at 120 degrees to the adjacent ones, means that only a single arm can be attached to the base. One arms therefore links to a series of jumper plates while the others rest on the tiles that make up the podium on which the tower stands. The round bricks that stand on this base are built up vertically, without any link to their neighbours. This method of construction could have made a model that would be weak and not hold together very well, so the artist included structural elements such as aerials and sticks threaded through the round bricks, plus an additional LEGO Technic rotor, part-way up the tower, to link the sections together horizontally. These elements give the tower greater structural integrity while having a minimal impact on the appearance of the model.

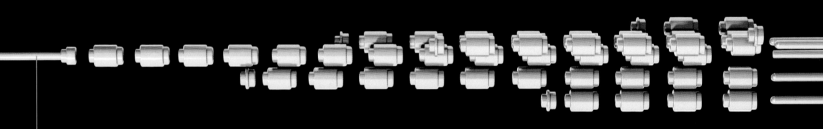

A whip-aerial forms the topmost tapering part of the tower.

The central part of the tower contains a stick with flange that fits into the hole at the centre of the rotor.

A three-blade rotor forms the structural core of the bottom of the tower.

A row of five jumper plates provides connection points to link the tower to the base.

Burj Khalifa

Whip-aerial components give structural strength to the outer sections of the building.

The studs on 1x3 plates placed on top of the rotor provide the anchor points for the nine separate outer sections of the tower.

**Shining Surfaces**
The facades of the tower are finished to a beautifully smooth surface, with no horizontal protrusions. The reason for this is that the atmosphere in Dubai contains fine dust that gathers on any ledge. The smooth surfaces help keep the building pristine.

# THE ORIGINAL

When Dubai's government and the ruling Sheikh Mohammed bin Rashid Al Maktoum decided to develop their city as a centre for commerce and tourism and reduce its reliance on oil revenue, they wanted a landmark building like no other. They commissioned Skidmore, Owings and Merrill, among the world's most prestigious architects of skyscrapers, to design the tallest building in the world. The architects responded with Burj Khalifa, a supertall skyscraper with a unique tapering shape. They based its structure on the bundled tube system developed in the Willis Tower (see p.182), Chicago, but added a buttressed core, which forms the hexagonal structure that supports the building's Y-shaped form.

From the core, which sits on 50-m-deep foundations, the tower's three wings rise to a total height of 827.9 m. The tower has a series of offsets arranged in a spiral pattern around the building, which give the tower its special form and help the structure cope with the huge wind load. The spire was added to the design once construction had begun, to improve the overall shape of the building.

**Dominating the City**
The vast tower reaches more than half a mile into the sky, making a show-stopping landmark in downtown Dubai. Its generous floor space contains more than 1,000 apartments, 49 floors of office space, a hotel, four swimming pools and the world's highest mosque. The double-decker lifts are among the world's fastest.

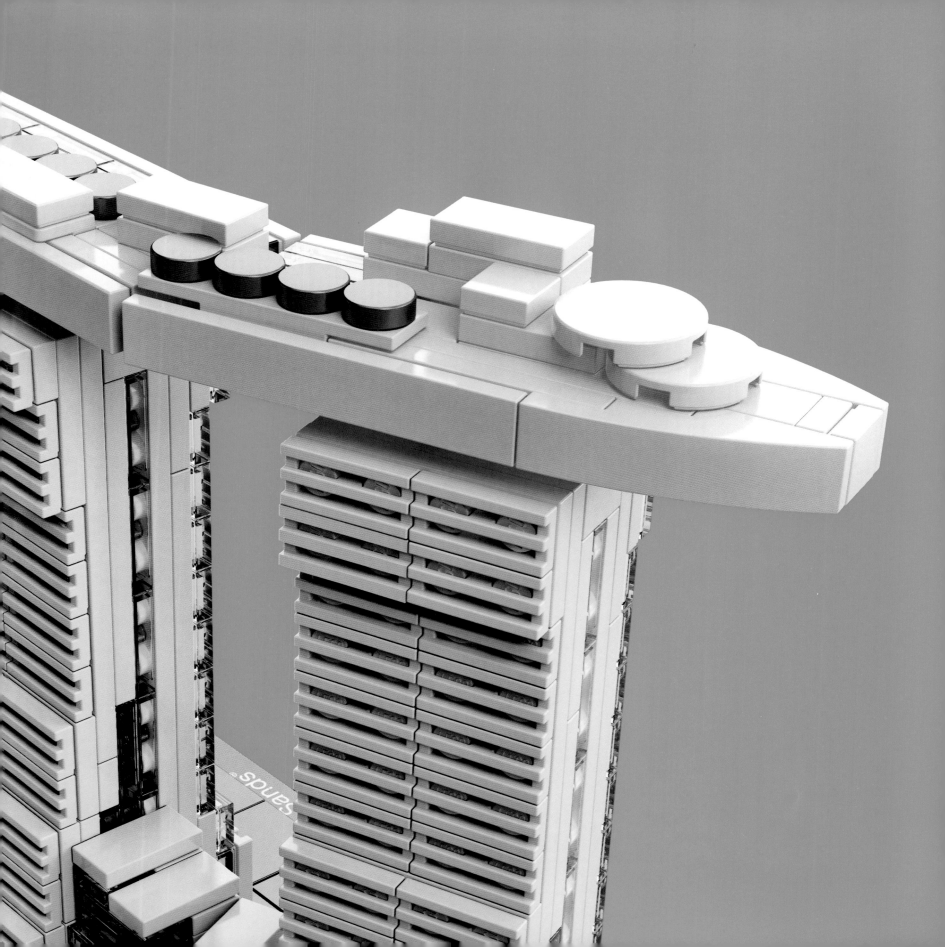

223

## Glazing Effects

The building has glazed facades that sweep from close to ground level right up to the structure of the Skypark. These glass fronts reflect the colour of the sky and the sea, making them appear blue in daylight. This impression of blue is captured in the LEGO® model with the use of transparent blue tiles with their flat surfaces facing towards the front. The tiles are attached to white plates, the studs of which are visible through the tiles. The rows of studs give the impression of the building's rows of windows.

Marina Bay Sands®

# MARINA BAY SANDS®

## LEGO® Artist: Rok Zgalin Kobe

Marina Bay Sands is an entire resort in a single
building. It contains a hotel, conference facilities,
entertainment venues, restaurants, shops, a casino,
and even a park set at the top of the building, about
200 metres above the ground. The main challenges
for Rok Zgalin Kobe, the LEGO® artist who designed
the model, involved recreating the building's many
curved surfaces and facades. At ground level the
three main towers are set in a curving formation,
the main facades all have a concave shape, and
the Skypark at the top curves like a vast banana.
The model recreates these curves mainly by using
steps and setbacks – there are very few actual
curved LEGO bricks in the model. The reason for
this is to do with the scale, and recreating the
enormous building at a small size posed another
challenge. Although the sweeping facades of the
towers have a uniform appearance that is not
difficult to capture in miniature, the Skypark and
other areas contain many elements that could easily
disappear in a small model. The artist managed to
suggest the long swimming pool, the trees that
grow on top of the building and other elements
of the Skypark by carefully selecting LEGO bricks
in blue, green and white, so that the model
embodies some of the features that make
Marina Bay Sands such an amazing building.

The building rises dramatically above the waters of Marina Bay.

**Building** Marina Bay Sands®
**Architect** Safdie Architects
**Location** Singapore
**Building type** Integrated resort
complex
**Year** 2007–2010

**Construction type** Steel and
reinforced concrete
**Height** 195 m
**Square footage** 9,096,000 sq. ft
**Architecture style** Modern

# THE MODEL

Having settled on a scale that represents roughly five storeys with one LEGO stud, Rok Zgalin Kobe built up the glazed facade with blue transparent tiles facing outwards, using the SNOT technique. Grille bricks cover the rear facade, which features rows of concrete balconies. The way in which the towers are set at an angle meant that only the central tower could be anchored to the base. Protruding studs on the base and overlapping bricks at the top of prevent the hinged towers from moving so that they retain their positions, true to the angled arrangement of the real building.

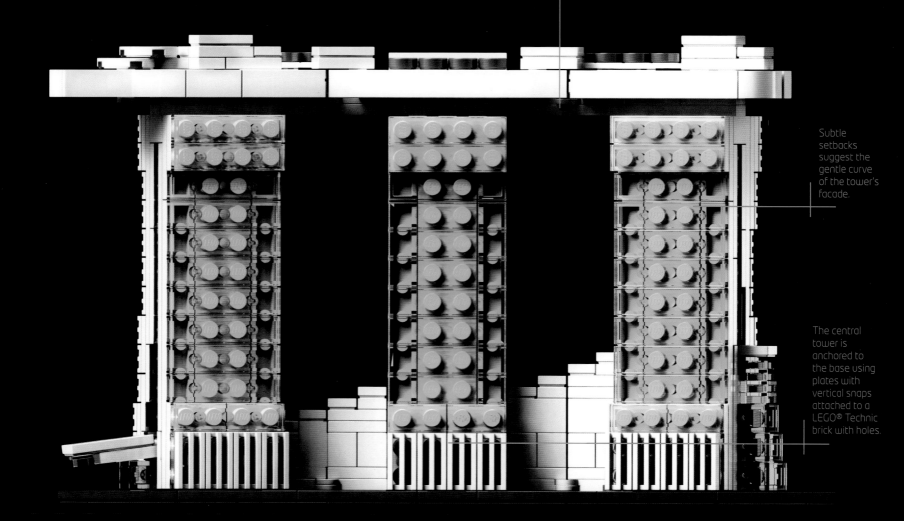

Hinged plates allow the three sections of the building to be joined at an angle.

Subtle setbacks suggest the gentle curve of the tower's facade.

The central tower is anchored to the base using plates with vertical snaps attached to a LEGO® Technic brick with holes.

**Model 21021**
Although it is small in scale, the LEGO model packs in detail by using many small bricks.

LEGO Architecture

**Marina Bay Sands®**
Republic of Singapore

Limited Edition

12+
21021

Landmark Series
Sehenswürdigkeiten
Série Monuments
Serie Monumental
Série Edifícios Históricos
Nevezetes helyek sorozat
乐高°建筑系列之地标系列

Model designed by
Rok Zgalin Kobe

**LEGO artist** Rok Zgalin Kobe
**LEGO builder** Jørn Kristian Thomsen
**LEGO bricks** 602
**Building steps** 36
**Dimensions** 224 x 136 mm
**Release date** 2014

The curved, overhanging end of the Skypark is formed using this 1x4 brick with bow, one of the few curved elements in the model.

Groups of green round tiles symbolise the many trees planted in the Skypark.

The swimming pool running along the edge of the Skypark is recreated using transparent blue tiles.

A brick with arch forms the corner of the straight end of the Skypark.

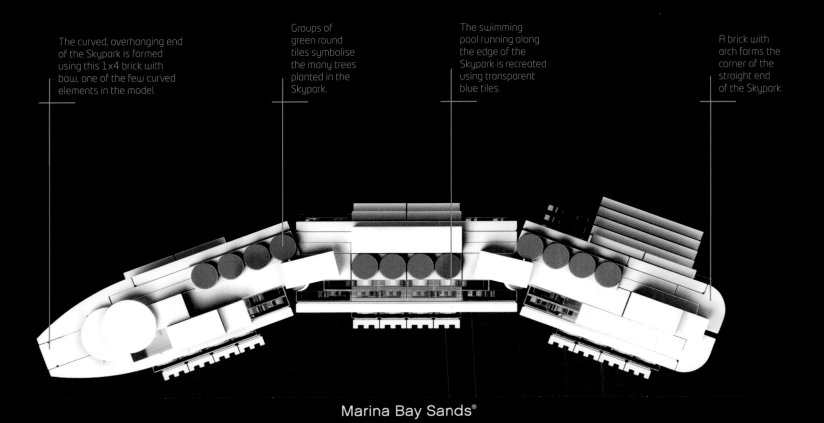

Marina Bay Sands®

**Moshe Safdie**
(b. 1938)
Safdie, an Israeli-Canadian architect, works in a modernist style, but is known for buildings that incorporate striking curved surfaces and that make notable use of green spaces. Since coming to prominence when he designed Habitat 67, a unique housing complex in Montreal, he has created buildings all over the world, from museums to city halls, universities to airports.

**Swimming to Infinity**
One of the main features of the Skypark is the infinity-edge pool, which is about 152 metres long and runs along the western edge of the building's top. Because this has no visible outer boundary, its water seems to abut directly on to the towers and lights of Singapore.

# THE ORIGINAL

Set on reclaimed land looking out over Marina Bay and Singapore's Central Business District, Marina Bay Sands acts as a visual focus in this part of the city. Its architect, Moshe Safdie, packed the towers, Skypark, and neighbouring structures with facilities, from a convention centre to a casino. At the heart of the complex is the hotel, with its rooms in the towers, looking out through the glazed west front and the eastern facade, which is covered with concrete balconies. The balconies are planted with bougainvilleas and these, together with the many trees in the Skypark, make Marina Bay Sands one of the most lavishly planted buildings in the world. Between the towers, at ground level, are structures full of shops, restaurants, entertainment venues and other facilities. Above are the gaps between the towers, which create vast "windows". Looking one way through the gaps reveals the densely packed city, and in the other direction there are views of the sea.

**Gateway to Singapore**
Standing on its peninsula of reclaimed land, Marina Bay Sands is almost surrounded by water. Whether reflecting the blue sky during the day or lit up at night as here, the building creates a symbolic gateway to the city.

# INDEX

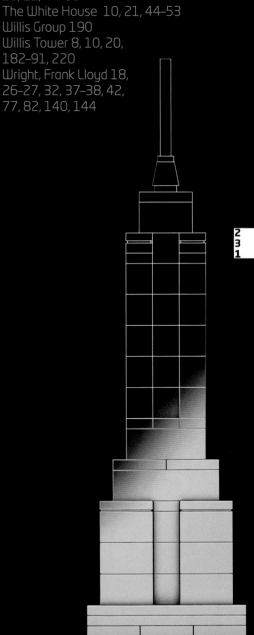

**DK**

LONDON, NEW YORK, MUNICH,
MELBOURNE AND DELHI

| | |
|---|---|
| SENIOR EDITOR | Victoria Taylor |
| EDITORIAL ASSISTANT | Beth Davies |
| SENIOR DESIGNER | Guy Harvey |
| PICTURE RESEARCH | Myriam Megharbi, Deepak Negi |
| PRE-PRODUCTION PRODUCER | Siu Chan |
| PRODUCER | Louise Daly |
| DESIGN MANAGER | Ron Stobbart |
| MANAGING EDITOR | Elizabeth Dowsett |
| ART DIRECTOR | Lisa Lanzarini |
| PUBLISHING MANAGER | Julie Ferris |
| PUBLISHING DIRECTOR | Simon Beecroft |

First published in Great Britain in 2014 by
Dorling Kindersley Limited
80 Strand, London WC2R 0RL
A Penguin Random House Company

10 9 8 7 6 5 4 3 2 1
001 – 184085 – 09/14

Page design copyright © 2014 Dorling Kindersley Limited

A CIP catalogue record for this book is available
from the British Library.

ISBN: 978-1-40935-572-4

Printed and bound in China by South China

**Discover more at
www.dk.com
www.LEGO.com**

## ACKNOWLEDGEMENTS

DK would like to thank Adam Reed Tucker for his huge contribution to
this book. Thank you also to Steen Sig Andersen, Rok Zgolin Kobe, Jorn
Kristian Tomsen, and Michael Hepp who all provided valuable information.
We would also like to thank Randi Kirsten Sorensen, Daiva Staneikaite,
and Marie Kjaer Buhl at the LEGO Group. The publisher would like to
thank Laura Nicholl, Helen Murray, Zoe Hedges, and Ruth Amos for
their editorial work, and Hilary Bird for the Index.

DK would also like to thank:
Frank Lloyd Wright Foundation (Solomon R. Guggenheim Museum™,
Fallingwater®, Robie™ House, and Imperial Hotel); National Trust for Historic
Preservation (Farnsworth House); Tishman Speyer and the Rockefeller Group
(Rockefeller Center); Sydney Opera House Trust (Sydney Opera House™);
Fondation Le Corbusier (Villa Savoye); United Nations Outreach Division
(United Nations Headquarters); HEARN (John Hancock Center); U.S. Equities
Asset Management, LLC (Willis Tower); Empire State Realty Trust, Inc. (Empire
State Building); Space Needle LLC (Seattle Space Needle); Burj Khalifa (Burj
Khalifa); Marina Bay Sands PTE Ltd and Safdie Architects (Marina Bay Sands
Hotel).

Picture Credits
The publisher would like to thank the following for their kind permission to
reproduce their photographs:
(Key: a-above; b-below/bottom; c-centre; f-far; l-left; r-right; t-top)

27 SuperStock: Kord.com / age fotostock / © ARS, NY and DACS, London 2014. 32 Dreamstime.
com: © ARS, NY and DACS, London 2014 (tl). 33 Corbis: Rudy Sulgan / © ARS, NY and DACS,
London 2014. 37 Courtesy of Western Pennsylvania Conservancy: Robert P. Ruschak / © ARS,
NY and DACS, London 2014. 42 Courtesy of Western Pennsylvania Conservancy: Robert P.
Ruschak / © ARS, NY and DACS, London 2014 (tl). 43 Courtesy of Western Pennsylvania
Conservancy: © ARS, NY and DACS, London 2014. 47 Dreamstime.com: Alberto Dubini.
52 Dreamstime.com: Valentin Armianu (tl). 53 Corbis: Charles Smith. 57 Alamy Images: Alan
Weintraub / Arcaid Images. 62 Corbis: Alan Weintraub / Arcaid (tl). 63 Arcaid Images: Hedrich
Blessing / Chicago Historical Society. 67 Dreamstime.com: Leo Bruce Hempell. 72 Getty Images:
Tetra Images (tl). 73 SuperStock: age fotostock. 77 Getty Images: Raymond Boyd / Michael Ochs
Archives / © ARS, NY and DACS, London 2014. 82 Getty Images: Raymond Boyd / Michael Ochs
Archives / © ARS, NY and DACS, London 2014 (tl). 83 Dreamstime.com: Edmund Holt / © ARS, NY
and DACS, London 2014. 87 Dreamstime.com: Daria Angelova. 92 Dreamstime.com: Moucher (tl).
93 Dreamstime.com: Andersastphoto. 96 Dreamstime.com: Bevanward. 100 Corbis: Nature
Connect. 101 Corbis: Marcel Malherbe / Arcaid (tr). 105 Dreamstime.com: Kadirlookatme.
110 Dreamstime.com: Warren Gibb (tl). 111 Dreamstime.com: Tomas Marek. 115 Alamy Images:
Schütze / Rodemann / Bildarchiv Monheim GmbH / © ADAGP, Paris and DACS, London 2014
and © FLC / ADAGP, Paris and DACS, London 2014. 118 Alamy Images: Schütze / Rodemann /
Bildarchiv Monheim GmbH / © ADAGP, Paris and DACS, London 2014 and © FLC / ADAGP, Paris
and DACS, London 2014 (tl). 119 Alamy Images: Schütze / Rodemann / Bildarchiv Monheim
GmbH / © ADAGP, Paris and DACS, London 2014 and © FLC / ADAGP, Paris and DACS, London
2014. 123 SuperStock: Photononstop. 128 Corbis: Topic Photo Agency (tl). 129 Corbis: TongRo
Images. 133 Dreamstime.com: Adrian Alexa J. 136 Dreamstime.com: Darryl Brooks (tl).
137 Dreamstime.com: Iakov Kalinin. 140 Photoshot: JTB / © ARS, NY and DACS, London 2014.
144 Alamy Images: Photo Japan / © ARS, NY and DACS, London 2014 (tl). 145 Getty Images:
Hulton Archive / © ARS, NY and DACS, London 2014. 148 Dreamstime.com: Breakers.
152 Dreamstime.com: Mario Savoia. 153 Dreamstime.com: Zhukovsky (tr). 157 Dreamstime.com:
Ryan Duncan. 162 Dreamstime.com: Alvaroennes (tl). 163 Dreamstime.com: Tim De Boeck.
167 Corbis: Dallas and John Heaton / Free Agents Limited. 170 Alamy Images: Vladimir Khirman.
171 Corbis: Ocean (tc). 175 Corbis: Raimund Koch. 180 Corbis: Joseph Sohm / Visions of America
(tl). 181 Getty Images: Hisham Ibrahim / Photographer's Choice RF. 185 Dreamstime.com:
Giovanni Gagliardi. 190 Getty Images: Tomasito! / Flickr Open (tl). 191 Corbis: Robert Glusic.
195 Corbis: Pietro Canali / SOPA RF / SOPA. 200 Axiom Photographic Agency: Andrea Pistolesi /
Tips (tl). 201 Corbis: SuperStock. 210 Dreamstime.com: Alexandre Fagundes De Fagundes (tl).
211 Getty Images: Tyler Marshall / Rubberball. 215 Dreamstime.com: Mizedig. 220 Dreamstime.
com: Ruben Gutierrez (tl). 221 Dreamstime.com: Emanuel Corso. 225 Dreamstime.com: Tangjans.
228 Corbis: Stephen Morrison / EPA (tl). 229 Corbis: Massimo Borchi / Atlantide Phototravel

Images of Sydney Opera House appear with permission—Sydney Opera House Trust 2014.
The name and shape of Sydney Opera House are trade marks of the Sydney Opera
House Trust.